Major Spiritual Awakenings From Pentecost to Billy Graham

by

O. B. Crockett

First Fruits Press
Wilmore, Kentucky
c2015

Major Spiritual Awakenings From Pentecost to Billy Graham, by O.B. Crockett.

First Fruits Press, ©2015
Previously published: Louisville, Ky.: Herald Press, 1950?

ISBN: 9781621712626 (print), 9781621712633 (digital), 9781621712640 (kindle)

Digital version at http://place.asburyseminary.edu/firstfruitsheritagematerial/109/

Crockett, O. B. (Ophel Butler), 1878-
    Major spiritual awakenings from Pentecost to Billy Graham / by O.B. Crockett.
    124 pages ; 21 cm.
    Wilmore, Ky. : First Fruits Press, ©2015.
    Reprint. Previously published: Louisville, KY : Herald Press, [1950?].
    ISBN: 9781621712626 (pbk.)
    1. Evangelistic work. 2. Revivals. I. Title.
BV3790 .C7 2015   248.5

Cover design by Wesley Wilcox

asburyseminary.edu
800.2ASBURY
204 North Lexington Avenue
Wilmore, Kentucky 40390

First Fruits
THE ACADEMIC OPEN PRESS OF ASBURY SEMINARY

First Fruits Press
The Academic Open Press of Asbury Theological Seminary
204 N. Lexington Ave., Wilmore, KY 40390
859-858-2236
first.fruits@asburyseminary.edu
asbury.to/firstfruits

MAJOR SPIRITUAL AWAKENINGS

FROM

PENTECOST TO BILLY GRAHAM

By

O. B. CROCKETT

Price: Single copy, $1.00, postpaid.
In lots of 10 or more copies on consignment
50 cents each, postpaid

Order From

REV. O. B. CROCKETT
240 McDowell Road
Lexington, Kentucky

THE HERALD PRESS
Louisville, Kentucky

INTRODUCTION

Dr. O. B. Crockett, the author of this timely book, has given more than a half century of service to the Christian ministry in the Methodist Church. He has always kept the true spirit of Revivalism in his ministry and this book is the fruition of many years of study and wide reading in this field. He convincingly demonstrates in this book that the history of Revivals has truly been the history of the Church. Many able authors and historians have discussed various phases of this study and definite periods, but I know of no one volume in all our evangelistic literature that covers the field as comprehensively as this. He demonstrates that from the time of King Josiah to Billy Graham and the present, that the Spirit of the Living God has worked and is working in true Revivalism. Certainly the history of the Church cannot be written without giving large space to the upsurge in its life that has come through the Revivals.

Evangelism is a very popular word today. There is danger in a word becoming so popular that the essential worth of its meaning evaporates into vagueness. True evangelism will always have Revivalism as one of its essential features. This book could well be called a modern apology for the true spirit of Revivals in the past and present. The author mentions very favorably every type of evangelism that is used in the modern world, but he demonstrates the strategic place that revivals have occupied in the history of the Church from the Old Testament times to the present. No one can thoughtfully read this book and not become convinced that God has truly worked through the revivals of the past and is active in

4

INTRODUCTION *(Continued)*

the present. He convincingly presents the truth of the Holy Spirit working in and through revivals.

I would especially urge my Ministerial Brethren to use this book as a basis of study for a revival in their own churches. Our laymen need the large perspective in regard to the place of revivals in the Church. This book will give them just that. Dr. Crockett carefully evaluates the good points in revivals and yet has not neglected to mention some of the unfavorable criticisms. Revivals should be judged by their total impact upon the Church and the world.

He gives a critical evaluation of the well-known Billy Graham, that is fair and candid. His chapter on the current revival is one of the best that I have seen. He clearly shows that the deep underlying current of the present revival is true to God and His Church and will bring a real spirit of righteousness in the world. In his closing chapter, he undertakes to tell us the kind of Revival needed today. He demonstrates that a real revival will bring forth abundant fruitage in moral and spiritual values both individually and socially.

I certainly hope that this book is widely read. I would like for some benevolent layman to send a copy of this book to every evangelical preacher in America. I predict that it will do inestimable good.

Russell R. Patton
Pastor, Epworth Methodist Church
1015 North Limestone Street
Lexington, Kentucky.

AUTHOR'S FOREWORD

It shall be my purpose in this book to focus attention upon mass evangelism, and to make a candid appraisal of its spiritual values.

I am fully aware that evangelism is a term with many facets. Its over-all meaning has to do with the spread of the gospel of Christ. There are several approaches to this divinely appointed task. Widely used techniques have evolved over the years. But it is an indisputable fact that practically all of the methods used today were used by Jesus and the early Christians. Paul expressed the attitude of the early Church when he wrote, "To all men I have become all things, to save some by all and every means."

In well planned revival efforts all known methods are used. In a significant sense a genuine revival marks the climax of the desire of Christians to win others to Christ.

It is my purpose to follow the revival stream from King Josiah to Billy Graham, and to discuss in chronological sequence, the great revivals that have moved the souls of men and kept the church on the march. In my rather extensive reading in this field, I have not seen a book that treated this important subject as I have attempted to do.

It is my belief that a summation of spiritual revivals of all times, given without excessive detail, will broaden the understanding and deepen the appreciation of all who will read the record. It is crystal clear that if the revivals cited had not occurred, our religion would not have the prominent place in the thought and life of men it has today.

I do not pretend that what this book contains will have the attraction of novelty, but I believe it will have reader appeal for all Christians who desire a fuller knowledge of revivalism as it has been expressed over the years.

Deep inside me has crystallized the conviction that the basic concept of revivalism belongs to the divine economy and that it is a fruitful means of keeping religion alive in the souls of men and in the life of the world. This conviction did not form while I was dwelling in an ivory tower. It came while I was in the midst of spiritual conflict. I was converted in a revival. I have closely observed the results of revival efforts in churches. I have served as minister over the years, and I have witnessed the conversion of sinners, as well as the inspirational boosts given to the churches.

I am sending this book forth with the earnest hope that all who read it will re-think and re-appraise revivalism, and that they will become vigorous supporters of this time honored method of making converts to Christ and His kingdom among men.

TABLE OF CONTENTS

CONTENTS *(Continued)*

ACKNOWLEDGMENTS

Before Doctor Albert Schweitzer wrote "Paul and His Interpreters," he read ninety-six lives of Paul by able writers; and before he wrote his "Quest of the Historical Jesus," he read sixty-eight Lives of Jesus by eminent scholars. When writing he constantly consulted these books and drew heavily upon them for information.

Many books have been written on spiritual revivals and I have read a great many of them. But these books have been passed on to schools and young preachers, and under the circumstances I shall be unable to give credit to whom credit may be due. But I do wish to acknowledge my great indebtedness to many who have written in this field, and to express my grateful thanks.

My good friend, Doctor R. R. Patton, graciously responded to my request to read the book and write the Introduction. He is the minister of a large and fast growing city church, and has to make the very most of his time, and I wish to express my deep appreciation of his generous action and helpful service.

CHAPTER I

REVIVALISM: A CONTROVERSIAL SUBJECT

Revivalism is not regarded with favor by many sincere Christians. Manifold objections are urged against it. They approve a revival of learning and art, trade and political action, and at the same time overlook the fact that the revival principle has religious uses and applications. It is passing strange that mass evangelism in the light of all that it has accomplished, should arouse so much criticism and opposition.

Every notable revival from Pentecost to the current revival has provoked heavy criticism and produced ridicule. There have always been those who have taken an exceedingly dim view of any unusual spiritual phenomena. Apparently they have not objectively analyzed revivals, and duly considered competent observers in this field, and checked varying views against each other for relative worth; and, I think it fair to presume that many who criticize revivalism are controlled by their prejudices and fixed opinions and are not qualified to make impartial observations and arrive at an unbiased and sound judgment.

Those who rejected Jesus did not believe that the disciples of the crucified Savior could promote a spiritual revival in Jerusalem. When the revival actually occurred, and thousands were converted and filled with the joy of the Holy Spirit, the unbelievers tried to discredit it by declaring it was nothing more than an orgy of drunkenness.

Evangelist Billy Sunday had many ardent admirers, and he also had many harsh critics. An able writer, Bruce Barton, was strongly opposed to Mr. Sunday, and following the evangelist's successful campaign in Philadelphia, Mr. Barton went to Philadelphia to expose and in every way discredit the evangelist. After investigating the revival results, and talking with the leaders of the city, Mr. Barton was convinced that the work accomplished was of God, and instead of writing an article of condemnation, he wrote and had published one of highest praise and endorsement.

Dr. Horace Bushnell was opposed to sporadic spiritual quickenings, or revivals, because he believed they were contrary to the "Christian Nurture" principle, which he so ably advocated. But we have discovered since the passing of this great and good man nearly a hundred years ago, that "Christian Nurture" and revivals belong together, each supplementing the other. In fact a successful revival is made possible by Christian nurture provided by the home, the Sunday School, and other cultural agencies.

The attitude of Doctor Bushnell toward revivals is not easily understood when we consider the fact that he did not have a conversion experience until he was nearly thirty years of age. He received a faithful Christian nurture in the home and he manifested a tender susceptibility to religious truth, but he did not make a public profession of his faith in Christ until he was nineteen years of age. About ten years later, when he was a student at the Yale Law school, a powerful revival came upon the college, and he was thoroughly re-born. As a result of his spiritual birth he exchanged the law for the

Christian ministry, and became one of the nation's greatest leaders.

It has been said that revivalism while successful during our pioneer days and among the unenlightened is not suitable to our advanced cultural life. This claim is completely refuted by the fact that some of the greatest revivals of the past were held in communities of the highest culture. Mass evangelism has done remarkably well in many centers of higher education.

The results of a revival effort are not always predictable. Sometimes the power of God "breaks through," spiritual tides run high, spill over into the community's life, and many are converted. At other times there is a numbing spiritual coldness throughout the services and the results are disappointing. Most of our revival failures may be traced to a lack of prayer and careful planning. Dedicated Christian workers, supported by the Holy Spirit, can throw the gospel net out over a community with the full assurance that they will reap a harvest of souls.

Some revival efforts do not produce the expected fruits and as a result there are those who develop an attitude of undisguised coolness. But an occasional failure should not cause men to have serious doubts relative to the merits of revivalism which God has signally blessed over the years in the salvation of lost humanity.

Many who unite with our churches during a revival soon fade from sight. This is why some oppose the revival. But Jesus saw the crowds melt away, and he continued his labors. All who came to Jesus did not go away. Some stayed and became apostles and martyrs. I have witnessed the conversion of many who became pillars in the church of God.

We cannot in fairness discredit revivalism because some of the work is superficial and because some of the converts do not continue faithful. Statistics are on the side of revivalism. A large majority of our church members and most of our preachers and missionaries were recruited during revivals.

A few years ago revival meetings did not draw the crowds and arouse the interest as they had formerly done. It looked as if the revival was on the way out. Well meaning Christians were ready to believe that the revival had served its day and should be discarded. During the same period political leaders decided that political barn-storming and extensive speaking tours were outmoded and should be abandoned. But times and conditions have changed again. Political mass meetings are drawing the crowds today. Massive political rallies have reappeared and monster political carnivals have become popular again. Large gatherings have voter appeal and political leaders would not consider dispensing with them.

The Master said to his disciples, "The children of this world are in their generation wiser than the children of light." But in this particular case leaders of the Church are as wise as the politicians. The Church, too, believes in mass appeal, and it is being used as never before, and with pronounced success. A soul stirring revival has gravitational force. It attracts the attention and arouses the interest of the indifferent and draws them to the place of meeting. This is especially true when sinners are converted. John in his Gospel tells us that many came to the home of Martha and Mary, not to see Jesus, but to see Lazarus whom Jesus had raised from the dead. Thus it has ever been. When the miracle of conversion takes place, when the spiritually dead are raised into newness of life, the people naturally move toward the place where the transformation took place.

There are those who are skeptical about revivalism because of its emotional features. The joyful expression of a happy Christian experience they regard as mass hysteria, or an emotional spasm, or a form of odious exhibitionism. In other public gatherings it is perfectly all right to express interest and enthusiasms with a loud noise; but if you attend a revival and receive the "joy that is unspeakable and full of glory," you cannot express this joy above a whisper without the raising of eyebrows.

The Christian religion is a happy religion. When Pliny lifted the curtain off of the early church, he found the Christians singing. They have been singing ever since. As long as pure and undefiled religion remains on this earth, there will be joy in the hearts, and songs on the lips, of the children of God.

In this connection we should recognize the fact that one's outward reaction of any experience of God will largely be determined by his temperament and cultural background. I feel that it is necessary to discourage excessive emotionalism and fanatical behavior, but in doing so, we must not forget that when "God's love floods our hearts through the Holy Spirit," we experience the sublimest passion that ever glowed in the human breast, and joyful expression is always in order.

It sometimes happens in our cities that when conservative congregations are observing a period of spiritual emphasis, they are visited by members of extreme religious groups who try to type the services by their noise and erratic conduct. This is a deplorable condition and if it is not corrected, will defeat the purposes for which the services were planned.

Professional evangelists, who are approved by their respective denominations, have been unjustly criticized. Unkind critics have accused them of commercializing a sacred calling. Generally considered, this charge is groundless. They receive less pay for their services than any other group of workers among us. Our evangelists are dedicated men, and their income for the most part is small; they belong to the church and are ready to serve when and where called; they bring to our churches gospel warmth, enthusiastic endeavor, and a crusading zeal. God has called these men and He needs their services. The churches need the "know how" and uplift they are prepared to give. They are brethren in the Lord and deserve our love and confidence, our prayers and our sympathy.

In the early Christian Church there were evangelists as distinguished from Apostles, prophets, pastors and teachers. The evangelists were travelling missionaries and publishers of glad tidings. They moved from place to place, winning the unsaved to Christ, and prepared the way for the pastors and teachers who followed up the work and made it secure.

An attempt has been made in this chapter to appraise some of the criticisms raised against mass evangelism. It is my belief that those who oppose this method feel that they have sound reasons for doing so. These critics do not have a hidden motive, and they are not creating a smoke screen in order to attempt a smothering blitzkrieg against revivalism. They have "honest doubts" which concise statistics and corroborative evidence have not dispelled.

Church historians with clear perspective and who understand spiritual manifestations on the scale of generations and centuries, have appraised revivalism and made clear the important contribution it has made to the life and progress of the Church. Present day trends indicate that revivalism is rapidly gaining in popular favor. It is not on the way out. It is on the way up. Critics may nibble and quibble; but they will never get rid of it. It will abide as long as the tides of the sea ebb and flow.

In spite of the strong under-current of honest criticism directed against mass evangelism, it is the belief of many persons who have carefully studied its aims and results, that this method of evangelism deserves top priority. Revivals have brought hope and strength to the Church in dark periods of its history, and they have been one of the decisive factors in brightening our present day outlook.

CHAPTER II

OLD TESTAMENT REVIVALS

In this chapter I shall give a sketch of three revivals recorded in the Old Testament Scriptures. A sketch does not imply a full account and complete analysis. Three revival episodes have been selected, which greatly affected the souls of men and the life of the Jewish nation.

It is significant that the ancient Jews had their spiritual ups and downs, even as later the Christians had theirs. At times the Jewish faith suffered severe setbacks and was threatened with utter extinction.

Medical experts tell us that when the heart suffers a coronary artery attack, the heart brings into operation its self repair circulation. Religious history makes plain the fact that the Jewish faith has a self repair system. At times of low tide God's rectifying influence became manifest, and their faith was revitalized, and the rivers of salvation began to flow again.

The current "Back to the Synagogue" movement among the Jews in this country has assumed mass proportions. Due to the "pogroms" in some countries many Jews were cruelly uprooted and scattered among friendly nations. Several million settled in this country, and after making the necessary economic and educational adjustments, they began to return to their synagogues from which they had become separated, and to seek satisfaction for their spiritual hunger. Jewish leaders report a large increase at public worship, and also an enriched religious observance in their homes.

20

A

REVIVAL UNDER KING JOSIAH

Josiah began to reign in Jerusalem when he was eight years of age, but he did not emerge into the light of history until he was eighteen years of age, at which time he restored the temple in Jerusalem, re-invigorated the faith of his people and turned them again to the worship of Jehovah.

Josiah was a pious iconoclast. He grew up as a religious reformer and purged Jerusalem and all Judah from idolatry. He realized that pagan religion had almost supplanted the worship of the true God. Idols were in evidence on every side, and his soul was stirred within him, and he sent forth his men with instructions to reduce to dust all idols wherever found. They did a good job. Not a false god nor a pagan idol was left in the land.

Next Josiah re-built the house of God, which had fallen into decay, and re-habilitated the worship of the Almighty.

When repairing the temple they found in the rubbish a copy of the book of the law, which had been lost for a long time. This may have been the whole Pentateuch or just one book of the law. In any event the reading of this book to the people caused the religious movement to take a more definite shape. The newly discovered book revealed to the people their sins and short-comings, and they repented and returned to the god of their salvation. The rites of their worship and service designated in the book of the law were re-instituted.

This Bible based revival brought to the people a religious reformation and a new tone to their national life.

It was a spiritual renaissance, a resurgence of the spirit and power of God in the life of men. This important episode in the life of the chosen people occurred about six hundred years before Christ, yet in many of its features it resembles spiritual revivals of the present day.

We can draw two important lessons from Josiah's revival: When a people become alienated from their religious traditions, they forget God, become the slaves of sin and victims of superstition. It was true twenty-five hundred years ago, and it is true today in a peculiar degree, that the success of a revival depends upon new encounters with the Word of God.

B

REVIVAL UNDER EZEKIEL

Ezekiel was one of the four greater prophets of the Jewish faith. Scholars in recent years have advanced numerous conflicting theories regarding this prophet and the book which bears his name. But they all agree that Ezekiel was a mystic of rare endowment and that he left a message which has had a profound influence on subsequent religious thought.

God's call to special service came to Ezekiel when he was with the Jewish captives on the banks of the Chebar, a river of Babylonia. No man was ever assigned a more difficult task than was he. His people were in political slavery and their faith had reached the breaking point. They hanged their harps upon the willows and refused to sing because there was no joy in their hearts. The phrase, "valley of dry bones" was symbolic of their spiritual and political condition.

After Ezekiel had been brought into this valley of death and saw the apparently hopeless condition of the people, the Lord said to him "son of man can these bones live? and the prophet answered, O Lord God, thou knowest." It is quite plain that the prophet did not have much faith in his mission, did not believe that he could accomplish the difficult task assigned to him. But Ezekiel was distinguished by his stern and inflexible energy of will and character, and when God commanded him to carry the divine vision and message to the people, he obeyed, and the people soon realized that there was a true prophet in their midst and a God in Israel.

The prophet began his work during a zero hour in the life of his nation. He was under divine orders to preach the truth whether the people heard him or not. This he did with outstanding courage and conspicuous success. At the end of twenty-two years of faithful ministry, and continuous effort, he witnessed the re-birth of his nation. New religious life and political hope appeared in this valley of death.

The work of the prophet provided an inspirational boost to the religious and political life of his people. It is a realistic assumption that without this God inspired revival, the Jewish people would have continued their hopeless existence in this valley of death into which their sins and forgetfulness of God had brought them. The prophet realized this, threw himself into the breach that the tragedy of his people might not deepen and their condition become increasingly hopeless.

C

REVIVAL UNDER NEHEMIAH

In considering Old Testament revivals, the striking spiritual awakening that came to the Jews in Jerusalem under the leadership of the prophet Nehemiah should be given high rating.

About the middle of the fifth century before Christ, invading Babylonians captured Jerusalem, reduced the city to ashes and carried the people into captivity. Later some of the captives were permitted to return to Jerusalem. But instead of keeping up their piety and patriotism, and fulfilling the purpose of God, they freely mingled with the pagans and adopted their manner of life. Consequently, they became corrupt in life and made no effort to restore their city which had been levelled by the invaders.

Messengers came to Shushan where Nehemiah was cup-bearer to the king, and told him of the sad fate of the returned exiles in Jerusalem. The recital of the tragic conditions deeply affected the feelings of this eminently pious and patriotic Jew. He says, "When I heard these words I sat down and wept, and mourned certain days, and fasted, and prayed before the God of heaven." But he did more than weep and fast and pray. He went before the king and told him of the lamentable condition of his people in the city of his fathers, and sought his sympathy and support. He requested permission to return to Jerusalem, and authorization to draw upon the resources of the royal forests for any building material needed in rebuilding the city. The king fully complied with the requests made.

Arriving in the city Nehemiah made an inspection

tour. He moved about incognito. By a careful survey
he verified the report made to him at Shushan, after which
he assembled the people of the city and told them what
he planned to do, with the approval of the king, and under
the guidance and blessing of God. And the people answered, "Let us rise and build."

The Jewish exiles who had returned to Jerusalem had
been given permission to repair the temple and their
private homes, but they were forbidden to rebuild the
walls of their city which the invaders had reduced to a
mass of shattered ruins. Nehemiah had been authorized
by the king to re-build the walls, and this he undertook
to accomplish. But as soon as the good work started, the
foreign element in the city led by Sanballat, Tobiah, and
Geshem, organized their forces and vigorously opposed
the building enterprise. They derided the workers and
accused them of rebelling against the king. But Nehemiah
knew how to deal with their opposition and ridicule, and
he said to them, "The God of heaven, he will prosper
us; we his servants will arise and build: but you have no
portion, nor right, nor memorial, in Jerusalem."

When ridicule did not halt the work, the enemy
resorted to force and threatened to reduce the city to a
shambles if the work continued. When Nehemiah was
informed of their evil plan, he mounted an effective defense system, assuring the people that the Lord was on
their side. The enemy did not attack.

After ridiculing and the threat of force failed to
slow down the workers, the ingenious enemy tried cunning.
They invited Nehemiah to meet them outside the city
under an armistice arrangement that they might discuss
the situation and arrive at some kind of a compromise. But

the prophet knew their treacherous designs and refused to comply with their request. He sent them the following message, "I am doing a great work, so that I cannot come down. Why should the work cease, while I leave and come down to you?"

The enemy, now desperate, made a final effort to defeat the work by attempting to discredit the leader in the eyes of the people. They informed Nehemiah that there was a plot to kill him and that he should flee to the temple for safety. But he refused to enter the temple for refuge, and provide his enemies cause for giving him an evil name, and taunting him because of his cowardice.

In spite of the malignant enemy and the dangerous stratagems they used to defeat the project, within the space of fifty-two days the walls of the city were re-built. This was made possible because of the impassioned devotion and consummate courage of the prophet and his supporters.

The nations around Jerusalem began to show respect for the strength displayed in the achievement. Furthermore, they knew that this prodigious work could not have been accomplished without the help of God. The national spirit of the Jews was re-awakened and they became politically strong. But what was more important, Nehemiah led his people back to God. Under the leadership of this man of high religious principle and patriotic spirit, the Jewish people entered into a new experience of God and a new vitality became manifest in the Jewish Commonwealth.

When Nehemiah returned to Jerusalem he found spiritual and political desolation. The divinely appointed agencies intended to keep the souls of men alive had been practically abandoned. The temple services had ceased and religious duties fallen into neglect; the Sabbath was profaned, the tithe withheld, and the word of God forgotten. The Jews had mingled with foreigners until they had almost lost their identity as a people. Their priests had become corrupt and religion as a vital force in their lives did not exist. The situation was characterized by hopelessness and despair.

Nehemiah proved that he was equal to the large task assigned to him. By his tireless and fearless service and with the assistance of Ezra the priest, and many others, Jerusalem became a new city. Walls of protection were rebuilt around it. The temple was cleansed, the divine law was active again, the tithe began to flow into the temple, and there was a re-kindling of the flame of piety. The Sabbath was restored to its sanctity, and their ancient covenant with God was renewed. The people solemnly promised God that they would cleanse themselves from everything foreign and walk in his holy ways. And God, as always, was merciful and kind, and He pardoned their sins of apostasy and uncleanness, healed their backslidings, and restored them to his love and favor.

What happened to the Jews during this brief period of twelve years, under the leadership of Nehemiah, marked one of the major turning points in the destiny of the chosen people, and may be regarded as one of the major revivals of the ancient Jews.

Able Bible scholars claim that a history of the ancient Jews can be written by writing the story of the great religious awakenings which they experienced along the way of their pilgrimage. At those times when they strayed from God's paths, lost sight of the ancient landmarks set up by their fathers, and forgot their divinely appointed mission, God would intervene, call them to repentance, and restore unto them the joy and strength of his great salvation. God's promises given through Solomon to his people standeth sure, "If my people, which are called by my name, shall humble themselves and pray, and seek my face, and turn from their wicked ways; then will I hear from heaven, and forgive their sins, and heal their land."

The Old Testament Scriptures close on a note of revivalism. John the Baptist belongs both to the Old and the New Testament dispensations. He is regarded as the last of the Old Testament prophets and the first of the New. He began his ministry by calling the people to repentance. His fame spread among all classes, and multitudes came to him to confess their sins, and to hear the message he brought from God. He stirred the people so deeply that they thought he was the Messiah, and they were ready to recognize him as such.

His brief ministry was brought to a close by his imprisonment, soon after which he was beheaded. His testimony to the divine nature and offices of Christ was full and distinct, and Christ pronounced John the greatest of the prophets. He brought to the multitudes who came to hear him a pungent sense of their sins and a new awareness of the presence of God. He prepared the way of the Lord.

Note: As the Jewish Commonwealth ideally considered was a theocracy, and as the civil and religious life of the people closely intermingled, Old Testament writers when recording their revivals and their results, made no distinction between the nation and religion. Jewish revivals, directly and equally influenced, both the civil and religious life of the Jewish people.

CHAPTER III

New Testament Revivals

In the previous chapter we considered three of the outstanding revivals recorded in the Old Testament Scriptures. In this chapter three of the major revivals recorded in the Acts of the Apostles will be considered.

A

THE REVIVAL IN JERUSALEM

Just before our Lord disappeared from the sight of his assembled disciples on a mount called Olivet, he instructed them not to depart from Jerusalem until the promise of the Father was fulfilled in them.: "John baptized with water but before many days, you shall be baptized with the Holy Spirit."

After the Ascension, the disciples returned to Jerusalem and entered an upper room and with one accord devoted themselves to prayer. They numbered about a hundred and twenty. After ten days of prayerful waiting, the promise was fulfilled and they were all filled with the Holy Spirit, and began to speak as the Spirit gave them utterance. There were in Jerusalem at this time devout men from every nation under heaven representing the Jews of the dispersion and proselytes to the Jewish faith. They had come to participate in the feast of the Passover, which had been instituted to commemorate the sparing of the Hebrews when God smote the first born of the Egyptians.

This favorable setting for the outpouring of the divine Spirit was not accidental. There is reason to believe that it was divinely planned so that the many visitors in Jerusalem at the time might witness the mighty works of God, and carry the burning energy to every tribe of men. The enumeration given of the nations represented is evidently intended to convey the impression of the universality of the gospel of Christ.

As the multitudes witnessed the behavior of those who received the gift of the Holy Spirit, they reacted in different ways. Some were bewildered and perplexed, and wanted to know what it meant. Others sneered and said, "They are brim-full of new wine." The Apostle Peter could not allow the serious charge of drunkenness made against his brethren to go unchallenged. He understood the astonishment of the people, and was ready to answer reasonable questions, but when he and his friends were charged with indulging in a drunken debauch, he stood up along with the eleven and answered, "These men are not drunk."

Then the Apostle, the first Christian preacher, preached the first Christian sermon. He told the people that what they were witnessing was the fulfillment of the "long-promised Holy Spirit" which had been predicted by the prophet Joel. The preacher convicted them out of their own Scriptures, and proved to them to their satisfaction that Jesus the Nazarene was approved of God, and that he represented God's deliberate purpose. "This Jesus you encouraged wicked men to nail to the cross and murder; but death could not hold him, for God raised him from the dead as we can all bear witness."

When the people heard this message, it went straight to their hearts; and they said to Peter and the rest of the Apostles, "Brothers what are we to do?" This simple gospel message, preached with the Holy Spirit sent from heaven, cut them to the heart, pierced them through and through. It brought to them a vivid awareness of their sin and they showed eagerness to find a way of escape, and requested that a course of action be pointed out to them. The answer given to the multitudes, stricken with a sense of sin, was the same as has been given to sinners for the last nineteen hundred years: Repent of your sins and believe on the Lord Jesus Christ. Nothing can be added to this formula of salvation and nothing can be taken from it. It represents the Alpha and Omega of the Christian evangel.

Those who received the word, with its cutting edge and pricking point, were baptized, and there came forward that day about three thousand souls. This was a fitting inauguration of the New Kingdom, as an economy of the Spirit. The new converts devoted themselves to the instructions given by the Apostles, and to fellowship, breaking bread, and praying together.

The believers all kept together and shared all they had with one another. Out of glad hearts they praised God, and were looked upon with favor by all the people. And the Lord added to their number day by day those who were being saved. Meantime there sprang up in Jerusalem a community of believers who recognized Jesus as Savior and Lord, and a heart-binding fellowship that in time would spread itself over the whole Roman empire.

The first Christian revival in Jerusalem as recorded in the Acts of the Apostles had cardinal significance. It marked the birth of the Church of Christ and the divine power promised by Jesus was freely given and savingly expressed. The city was stirred from center to circumference and thousands were converted. A divine society was started which has continued with an ever increasing strength to the present hour. Many visitors in the city at the time were converted and carried the gospel message to their far away countries and prepared the way for the future extension of the Gospel of Christ. to the outermost rims of the earth.

This sweeping refreshing from the presence of the Lord in Jerusalem prepared Christ's disciples for the brilliant initiative which they immediately expressed. The conspicuous success and exciting progress of their cause aroused the vigorous opposition of the Jewish authorities. The apostles displayed heroic courage in their championship of the gospel of Christ. Angry threats and cruel persecution did not cause them to alter their course of action. When the rulers of the temple ordered them not to speak or teach a single sentence about the Name of Jesus, they answered, "Decide for yourselves whether it is right before God to obey you rather than God; certainly we cannot give up speaking of what we have seen and heard. One must obey God rather than man." They had a message to deliver, an evangel to declare, a Savior to make known and to share, and in spite of opposition they continued their good work with consuming intensity until Jerusalem was filled with the doctrine of Christ.

Measured by the graphic results achieved and the wide publicity given it, the revival in Jerusalem immediately following the baptism of the Holy Spirit on the day of Pentecost, will stand out for all time to come as the greatest and most far-reaching revival in human history.

B

REVIVAL IN SAMARIA

The promoter of the revival in Samaria was Philip, one of the seven deacons selected by the disciples in Jerusalem. He was swept out of Jerusalem on a wave of persecution that threatened to destroy the infant Church. He came to a city in Samaria and preached Christ to the people. How often has the rage of Christ's enemies "turned out rather unto the furtherance of the gospel." The Christ whom Philip uplifted drew large crowds to the services and the people with one accord gave heed to what Philip said. The Samaritans felt their need of a divine revelation and they were ready for religious guidance. Jesus had previously declared that this particular field was white unto the harvest and waiting for the reaper.

Philip's gospel mission to Samaria was a providential one. He was a Hellenistic Jew, and had been exposed to Greek speech, ideas and culture. There was a long standing antipathy between the Samaritans and the Jews. and a native of Judea would not have been cordially received by them. Samaria was a bridge between Jerusalem and the outside world, and the Jews found it rather difficult to pass through this ancient iron curtain. But Philip, because of his cosmopolitan culture and outlook, was qualified to preach the gospel to the Samaritans, and they gave him a polite hearing.

The ministry of Jesus extended into Samaria. He met a sinful woman at Jacob's well and talked with her about the things of God. This woman was the first to hear from the lips of Jesus the announcement that he was the Messiah. To her he spoke the revolutionary truth, "God is a Spirit; and they that worship him must worship him in spirit and in truth." This basic principle of worship enunciated by Jesus was calculated to raze the walls separating Jews and Samaritans, and in time to unite the worship of all peoples in the Spirit and reality of God.

When the disciples returned from the village where they had gone seeking food, and found Jesus talking with the woman, they marveled. The woman hurried into the city and said to the people, "Come see a man who told me all I ever did. Can this be the Christ?" The Samaritans went out to see Jesus, and when he saw them coming, he regarded them not as a despised people, but as a harvest field ripe for the harvest. The Samaritans urged Jesus to stay with them, and he stayed for two days. Many believed and accepted his teachings, and they said to the woman, "Now we believe, not because of thy saying: For we have heard him ourselves, and know that this is indeed the Christ, the Savior of the world."

It is significant that the most widely known and most frequently quoted parable of Jesus has a Samaritan as its hero.

When Philip arrived in Samaria he found that the soil had been prepared by Jesus, and that the people were ready for his message. The exact field of his labor in Samaria is not known. Some scholars think he did his evangelistic work in the capital city, others think it was in Sychar, and others think it was in some other place of large population. The important thing is that he went to Samaria and preached Christ to those who did not know him, and at some place where the divine society had not been established.

It is not known how long Philip preached Christ in Samaria, but it is known that the people with one accord gave heed to what he said. He promoted a revival of land-slide proportions. The whole city was stirred. Those who believed represented a large company, and they were delivered from the sins that had degraded their lives, and saved from the sorceries that had bewitched them, and they were clothed with new life and hope. "There was great joy in that city."

"When the apostles at Jerusalem heard that Samaria had received the word of God, they sent to them Peter and John, who came down and prayed for them that they might receive the Holy Spirit. They laid their hands upon them, and they received the Holy Spirit." This information is important in that it is in full harmony with the history of the rise and extension of the early Christian Church as recorded by Luke in the Acts of the Apostles. This book is regarded by some as the acts of the Holy Spirit. As this is the earliest authentic record of the beginning and development of the Church of Christ, it is highly imperative that due consideration be given to the primacy of the Holy Spirit in all that was said and done.

Philip, who was a lay evangelist, had received the gift of the Holy Spirit in Jerusalem, and the apostles were anxious that the Samaritan converts receive the same gift, that they might be qualified to carry forward Christ's cause in their country. Doubtless, Peter and John were deputized to appraise the work of Philip, and to organize a new Christian soceity. But their chief concern was that those who had accepted Christ receive the fulness of the blessing of Christ. Herein lies the secret of how the Christian faith went forth, conquering and to conquer.

About the time Philip's successful work in Samaria reached a climax a strange thing happened to him. A messenger of the Lord told him to leave the city where his hands were full of work and travel south on a desert road. As he was left in ignorance as to the object and purpose of his journey, it must have been staggering to his faith. But like Abraham of old he went forth "not knowing whither he went," and like Paul he "was not disobedient to the heavenly vision."

As he traveled under sealed orders in the appointed direction he came to a man riding in a chariot, reading the Scriptures. The man was from Ethiopia, and a Jewish proselyte who had traveled a thousand miles to Jerusalem to attend the Passover festival and to worship God. The Spirit said to Philip, "Go up and join this chariot." Philip ran to the man and "told him the good news of Jesus." The Ethiopian accepted Christ as his Savior, was baptized, and went on his way rejoicing. He found that Christ was the key to the Scriptures. His soul was set free and his discipleship sealed. He felt that he was a new man and his joy was full.

The Samaritan revival led by Philip emphasizes certain facts which we need to remember. Theologically considered, we would not have a trinitarian God without the Holy Spirit; but an experience of the Holy Spirit is vastly more important in the work of saving the world than is a satisfactory formula of Deity. "The letter killeth, but the spirit giveth life." Furthermore, this revival clearly points up the place o fmass evangelism and mass conversion in the Christian enterprise. And when Philip won the Ethiopians to Christ he provided us an example of individualistic evangelism. The approaches to the souls of men may be different, but the basic objectives are the same.

C

REVIVAL AT EPHESUS

Ephesus was the capital of the province of Asia in Asia Minor. It had the largest theater in the world, was considered one of the eyes of Asia, and was the center of a hundred thousand people. It was the home of the goddess Diana who had reigned as queen of the Ephesians for four hundred years, and had devotees all over the world. It took two hundred years to build this elaborate and costly shrine, and it was one of the seven wonders of the world. This shrine was made of pure marble and tribute was levied against the whole province for its building. Ephesus was honored with the charge of the temple, but thirteen cities of the province had an interest in it.

Ephesus was thoroughly steeped in pagan worship, sorcery, and witchcraft, and naturally it was not an inviting field of Christian endeavor. It would appear that a city of this character would prove impervious to the gospel message and that it would be well for the missionaries to by-pass it.

As Paul's home at Tarsus was not far from Ephesus, he was familiar with the city, and its superstitions, and he was willing to match the gospel power he represented against the pagan power of Ephesus. As he was going out on his second journey he attempted to stop at Ephesus, but the Holy Spirit forbade his doing so. Why he was

forbidden is not detailed by this historian. After he fulfilled his European mission, and while returning to Jerusalem, he stopped at Ephesus for a few days and preached
Christ in the Jewish synagogue. When invited by the
Jews to stay longer, he declined, but when departing he
said, "I will return to you if God wills."

After some time Paul returned to Ephesus as he had
promised and began at once to establish a strong base of
evangelistic activity. This city represented a supreme
challenge to the Christian faith, and the apostle possibly
felt that if the gospel could triumph in this heathen ridden
city, it could succeed any place else on the earth.

Paul was an able leader, and he knew that careful
planning was necessary to a successful spiritual campaign.
He knew he must discover and mobilize all available help.
He found that there were a dozen Christian believers in
the city, and he soon discovered that they knew nothing
of the power of God and were as helpless as soldiers without equipment. His plan called for a spiritual blitzkrieg,
a vigorous attack upon a wicked city, and Paul knew that
immature, uninformed, believers would be of little assistance.

When Paul asked the believers if they received the
Holy Spirit when they believed, they told him that they
had never heard of the Holy Spirit. He expounded unto
them the word of God more perfectly, after which he
laid his hand upon them and the Holy Spirit came upon
them. This seasoned campaigner knew the limitations
of their enlightenment and the cause of their weakness,
and now that his helpers had received divine power he
was ready to lay seige to the city and claim it for Christ.
The battle for the soul of the city lasted for about three

years. Paul came to Ephesus to perform an evangelistic task which needed to be done, and he had no thought of leaving until his mission was accomplished.

Paul and his helpers approached this task under the inspiration and guidance of the Holy Spirit. The substance of their message was the same as used elsewhere. They declared that Christ was the Messiah, and that salvation could be obtained by repentance toward God and faith in the Lord Jesus Christ. They not only conducted public services, but day and night, they visited from house to house, offering salvation through Christ unto all who could be persuaded to accept it.

The revival services began in the Jewish synagogue, but the rulers of the synagogue after a time, became abusive and it was necessary to hold the services in another place. Jews and Greeks alike responded to the gospel appeal, many believed, and the name of the Lord was magnified. Those who had practiced magical arts confessed and divulged their evil practices, and brought their books and wares together and burned them in the sight of all.

When the revival reached large proportions and began to affect adversely an important business interest, a new opposition to Paul appeared. The first opposition came from religious leaders, and now Paul finds that big business is organized against him and his cause. The silver-smiths who made and sold silver replicas of Diana realized that Paul was injuring their business by turning the people from idols to serve the living God. There was no market for their wares by which means they made their living, and they raised a hue and cry against Paul and his helpers. They gathered a mob bent on destruction, and filled the city with confusion. They were ready to destroy Paul and his companions, and doubtless would have done so, had not the civil authorities taken charge and restored order.

A dynamic spiritual revival is always hurtful to evil institutions. Moral cess-pools are filled up, and wrong is placed on the defensive. When men accept Christ's way of life they cease to encourage by their presence and patronage any business that destroys the moral and spiritual life of the community. The religion of Christ creates in men a sense of moral responsibility, and Christian men, if true to their high calling in Christ Jesus, must always take issue with their fellow-citizens when moral values are challenged by them.

The current revival in our country, before it reaches its crest, will focus upon the public mind our manner of national life as indicated by the way our people spend their money. The grim facts are that the American people spend twenty billion dollars a year on gambling, ten billion a year on liquor, seven billion a year on education, and three billion a year on religion!

This situation does not point toward a golden age for this Republic. On the contrary, it is a sure prophecy of the evil days which lie ahead, and are sure to come unless something of a radical nature is done to change the present situation.

The sweeping revival in Ephesus had missionary overtones. The revival discredited the most famous goddess in the world, ·turned her devotees from an idol to the living God, and greatly injured a business that was built upon greed and superstition. The revival also created a new missionary impulse. Ephesus became a radiating center of gospel light. They did not have present day means of communication but the gospel was carried forward on the feet of living witnesses until the entire province of Asia heard the good news of salvation. Many of the converts lived in places other than Ephesus, and they carried the gospel message to their families, friends, and neighbors. The city of Ephesus thus became a sounding board from which sounded forth the message of salvation to those in distant places. The city was made an ecclesiastical center and remained so for a long time.

CHAPTER IV

THE CHURCH'S GOLDEN AGE

The first two hundred years of the Christian era marked the golden age of the Church. This claim is fully supported by the extensive areas reached and the results achieved during this period.

The Christian movement began in Jerusalem on the day of Pentecost when the Holy Spirit was given. It began with a new fellowship built upon an experience of God. Men found in this new society warmth and strength, and as the years passed the ever widening circle of this fellowship reached peoples in distant places, and it brought benediction and hope to those touched by it. In its outward thrust and onward march the Christian movement crossed racial lines and cultural barriers, and geographical boundaries, and demonstrated that the Christian religion was universal in scope and eternal in application. The gospel message was carried forth by approved missionaries, and it was also carried to the world on the feet of tradesmen, emigrants, and soldiers, who had been initiated into the Christian fellowship.

Luke in the book of Acts gives a historical account of the rise and progress of the Christian movement during the first generation of Christians. This is one of the most fascinating books ever written. Luke lifts the curtain on a stirring drama, and those who read the early Christian story feel that they are reading about world shaping events.

The apostle Peter opened the door of hope to the

Jews in Jerusalem, and later to the Gentiles when he preached Christ to a Roman soldier. Evangelist Philip carried the gospel message to Samaria and had remarkable success in winning the Samaritans to Christ. Christian believers carried the glad tidings to the Gentile city of Syrian Antioch, where the message was cordially received. Many Jews of the dispersion lived in Antioch, and they had been Hellenized to the extent of adopting Greek speech, ideas and customs. These Jews were more susceptible to the Christian message than the Jews who lived in Palestine, and they became the nucleus of a strong Christian church in Antioch, and the center of the Christian movement was shifted from Jerusalem to Antioch. This wicked city was the mother of Gentile Christianity and it became a spring-board of missionary activity. Under the direction and inspiration of the Holy Spirit, Paul and Barnabas went out from the church at Antioch to preach Christ to the Gentiles. It was from Antioch that the Christian church moved westward.

Paul sparked and spear-headed the westward march of the Church. He was divinely guided all along the way. During his second missionary journey he attempted on two different occasions to depart from his appointed course; but the Holy Spirit guided him on an unbroken course until he arrived at Troas located on the Aegean Sea, where he was called through a divine agency to pass on to Europe. He was not disobedient to the heavenly vision. Paul had been called to be a missionary to the Gentiles, to turn them from darkness to light and from the power of Satan unto God, and when he was called to leave his native Asia and go to another continent, he immediately obeyed.

When Paul arrived in Europe he found that "the highest splendour of heathenism" had reached the end of its resources and had left the people "without hope and without God." It offered no answer to the deepest cravings of the immortal spirit within men and it did not possess sufficient power to rebuild shattered lives.

In the light of the Book of Acts, it is not difficult to assess the merits of the Christian faith and to explain its success. Paul and his fellow-missionaries represented a power not of this world. They were dealing with a desperate situation. The darkest word picture of sin ever written is found in the first chapter of Paul's letter to the Romans. But he told the Romans that he brought to them a potent remedy to meet their ills, that "the gospel is the power of God for salvation to every one who has faith, to the Jew first and also to the Greek."

The missionaries preached good news to the defeated and unhappy. They offered hope to the hopeless, warm friendship to the friendless, soul emancipation to the enslaved, salvation and a happy eternity to all believers. The people had never before heard a message like this, and we need feel no surprise that converts were made and the Christian Church established and supported.

As the Christian missionaries moved westward, they made converts all along their line of march, and like a well disciplined army they consolidated every position occupied. Cross after cross might be seen along the way marking the places where churches had been established. After a few years the Christian faith became such a strong force in the loyalties of Christian believers that this force had to be considered and reckoned with by the holders of temporal power. In less than three hundred years the banners of Christ were lifted over the imperial city of Rome, foretokening its universal triumph.

When I selected three revival episodes for discussion from the Book of Acts, it was far from my thought to leave the impression that other revivals were not taking place over the Roman empire during the period covered by the three discussed. The Christian Church was born in a revival and the spirit of revivalism was expressed in every place the Christians appeared. When the Christian missionaries arrived at Thessalonica in Greece, unfriendly citizens said, "These men who have turned the world upside down have come here also."

Medical doctors tell us that the heart in sending blood out to the furthest extremities of the human body has the assistance of booster stations along the way which enable it to fulfill its mission. Electric power is transmitted long distances after the same manner; and oil and gas are carried through pipe lines for thousands of miles by the use of auxiliary pumping stations. Rockets are sent into the stratosphere by a series of propelling explosions along the way of their travel.

In like manner the Christian faith passed from Jerusalem to the farthest reaches of the Roman empire. There were spiritual booster stations, or revivals, along the way of its march. New centers of operation were established and there were fresh outpourings of the Holy Spirit. Some of the revivals were conspicuous for their success and attracted wide attention; others were only local in their influence and attracted small attention. But it was true then as it is today that the small revival is important in its sphere of influence. It is possible that numerous small revivals prepare the field for the success of our noted evangelists.

It is apparent that revivalism was necessary to the extension of the early Christian enterprise. And in my judgment spiritual revivals are indispensable as long as there are teeming millions of earth unevangelized and unsaved.

The early Christian preachers offered to all men an experience of redemption in Christ on the condition of "repentance toward God and faith in the Lord Jesus Christ." This is the essence of all true preaching that has as its aim the conversion of sinners.

Luke informs us in the Book of Acts that water baptism was the unvarying practice of the early Church. He does not mention baptism in his Gospel, but in Acts he tells us that those who accepted Christ as Savior were baptized. Baptism was a mark of separation from heathen practices and former religious loyalties. It marked a break with the old manner of life, and it was a door of entrance into the divine fellowship. Baptism was a severe test for those converted from paganism, but it was pressed upon them as a present duty. Membership in the Christian society was necessary, and was not considered an optional matter, nor was it a debatable question. New converts were required to band themselves together with other Christians for fellowship, worship and service, and to meet all of the requirements of membership in the Church of Christ.

The Christians were persecuted from the beginning. "The blood of the martyrs was the seed of the Church." They were opposed by the Sadducees because of their victorious and happy faith in a future life. There is no record of a Sadducee accepting the Christian faith. The

Pharisees were more friendly to the Christians than the Sadducees and many of them accepted Christ. But as a ruling class they bitterly opposed Jesus because he publicly condemned their hypocrisies and cut across their prejudices. Jewish leaders of all parties obstructed the progress of the Christian movement to the full extent of their ability to do so.

Gentile persecution appeared later because the Christians showed contempt for pagan gods, and exhorted the people "to turn from their vanities and serve the true God only." The pagans branded the Christians "atheists" and enemies of their gods, and they persecuted them beyond measure. The Christians committed their greatest offense against the secular power when they refused to participate in emperor worship. From the reign of Nero to the reign of Diocletian, there were ten systematic persecutions, directed by the Roman government, whose expressed purpose was to exterminate the Christian faith. But the Christians refused to be intimidated by the threat of worldly force. They had a faith which the sword could not cut out, and which fire could not burn out, and the claws of wild beasts tear out. In spite of these cruel persecutions, they mastered the world without drawing a single sword in their own defense. The Christian Church continued triumphant until the conversion of Constantine which marked the water-shed between the Golden Age of the Christian Church and a diluted Christian faith, and greatly weakened church, which followed in the wake of Constantine the Great.

CHAPTER V

CONSTANTINE AND AUGUSTINE

This chapter is written to fill in the gap between the "Golden Age" of the Church and the twelfth century. This was a period characterized by ecclesiastical and political maneuvering; and there were no revivals that conformed to the accepted New Testament pattern.

When Constantine became sole emperor of the West in the early part of the fourth century, he accepted the Christian faith and identified himself with the Christian cause. The decisive battle for military power took place at Milvian Bridge near Rome and according to Eusebius an incident occurred before the battle which caused Constantine's conversion. He saw a flaming cross in the sky at noon day with the motto: "By this conquer." Whether this reported incident was true or false, he did become a champion of the Christian cause, and persecution ended.

As the first Christian emperor, Constantine endowed the new religion with an instrument of worldly power, which has been a thorn in its side ever since. This gave to the Church a popularity which drew into the membership unconverted multitudes. The high visibility of the Christian became obscured and it became difficult to distinguish the Christian from the non-Christian.

Before Constantine appeared on the scene the Church had reached unprecedented heights of spiritual power and influence. Its geographical expansion extended all over the Mediterranean world, and it had grass-root strength in places where the cross had been lifted. And it is strikingly significant that this accomplishment had been achieved without the imperial favor of Rome. On the contrary, the Church had prospered in spite of the organized and systematic persecution of Rome.

At the beginning of the fourth century the Christians represented the most stable and cohesive force in the Roman empire. The Christians were too numerous and too strong to suppress, and it is possible that Constantine decided that it would be an act of sound policy for him to join the Christians and annex the Church to his disintegrating empire.

The Christian religion at its beginning was a world-denying religion. Conformity to the world was forbidden. The Christians depended on their faith and the adequate merit of their cause for acceptance and success. "This is the victory that overcometh the world, even our faith."

This attitude toward the world was changed when Constantine annexed the Church to his world chariot. The simple forms and organization borrowed largely from the Jewish synagogue gave place to complicated forms, and organization molded after imperial Rome. This led to the spiritual paralysis of the Church, and doomed it to a futile existence. Instead of Constantine bringing strength to the Church, and assisting it in establishing the reign of God, his influence stopped it in its tracks in its march to complete world conquest. The patronage of the world has never done the Church any good. It has always been a source of weakness and corruption. All the Church asks of the state in a free society is to be left strictly alone.

Saint Augustine was converted when he was thirty-three years of age through the influence of Bishop Ambrose and the prayers of his godly mother. His monumental intellect and extensive abilities were fully dedicated to the cause of Christ, and he soon became the outstanding Christian leader of his day. He won many to Christ, and promoted a revival that reached large areas of North Africa. He served as Bishop of Hippo for thirty-five years, and to his honor, he exercised the functions of the episcopacy without seeking or accepting assistance from political rulers. Under his inspiring leadership the Church was built up to great strength in North Africa.

During the early part of the fifth century when Augustine was in the midst of his productive labors, the Roman empire began to totter on its foundations and to fall to pieces. The Goths conquered and sacked Rome and the Church suffered a staggering blow. When the Christians of North Africa heard that the barbarians were attacking their faith, they grew sad and despondent and felt that the end of the world was near.

It was during this crisis that Augustine produced his "City of God," in which he defended the workings of God's providence, and emphasized the solidity of the "city which hath foundations," and the instability of paganism.

But the vandals moved on from Rome to Africa and succeeded in devastating the Roman province where Augustine had done his mighty kingdom work. The remnant of the Christian Church left after the carnage of the vandals, was later destroyed by the invading Mohammedans. The Christian Church in North Africa has not yet recovered from the destruction wrought upon it by the vandals and the Mohammedans.

In the eleventh century the Christian Church was divided into two parts—East and West. About the same time the Crusades began and lasted for three hundred years. The expressed object of the crusades was to wrest holy places from the infidel. Vast armies were mounted and marched from Europe toward Jerusalem and the Holy Land. For the most part these armies became disorganized and disintegrated before they reached their destination.

The Crusades were called wars of the Cross against the Crescent. The volunteer soldiers who composed these armies turned a religion of love into a religion of hate and carnal strife. As far as the direct object for which the Crusades were undertaken is concerned, the Crusades must be regarded as total and signal failures.

CHAPTER VI

THE WALDENSIAN REVIVAL

Roughly considered the "Dark Ages" began shortly after Augustine and continued until the fourteenth century, which time in history marked the beginning of the Renaissance---the revival of art, letters, and learning in Europe. During this dark period of nearly a thousand years the only spiritual revival of historical importance occurred in southern France and northern Italy in the twelfth century under the leadership of Pierre Waldo, a rich silk merchant of Lyons.

Waldo received much inspiration from reading the Bible and the writings of the Church Fathers, and he determined to initiate a form of life patterned after the Apostles and early Christians. He gave his earthly goods to the poor and by his preaching collected numerous followers. Most of his converts came from a class of artisans who because of the place of their birth were called "Poor Men of Lyons."

Waldo and his followers were called Waldenses, which is the oldest Protestant body in the world. This sect has continued for nine hundred years, and it is believed that it will soon merge with the Methodist Church of Italy.

This new sect promoted a revival that rapidly spread over large areas of two nations. It was a lay movement. Dedicated laymen carried the gospel message to the poor and neglected, and led tens of thousands to Christ. These men set a pattern of aggressive evangelistic action which guided reformers of later times.

There were two groups of Waldenses, one in France and the other in Italy. While there are conflicting views as to the originator of the sect, most of the available sources point to Waldo as the founder. Especially is this true of the group that operated in and out of Lyons and were known as the "Poor Men of Lyons." Both in France and Italy, Waldo was recognized as the leader.

The Waldensian sect emerged as a protest against a corrupt church and priesthood, and it provided the first impulse for the reformation of the Christian Church. Like Luther and Wesley the Waldenses had no intention of leaving the church of their fathers. Rather they desired to reform the Church from within and remain in its fellowship. They held to the doctrines of the Church and went to Catholic sources for their literature, and to the priests for the sacraments. At the same time they vigorously expressed their contempt for the degenerate clergy and opposition to the Roman priesthood. After fifteen years of successful revival effort they were excommunicated by the Pope.

After the Waldenses were rudely driven from the Church of their childhood, they made the Bible alone the rule of their faith and practice, and rejected any teaching that was not supported by the Scriptures. They rejected the confession of the Church, and preached that a bad priest cannot validly administer the sacraments.

When the French Waldenses were practically stamped out by persecution, the Italian group took over the leadership of the movement. The sect thus separated from the Roman Church, abolished the confession, and recognized only two sacraments—baptism and the Lord's Supper.

The Waldenses were distinguished for their pure morals, industry and good citizenship. Their way of life rested entirely on the Gospels and apostolic teaching. By order of Waldo a new translation of the New Testament was made. They revived pure and undefiled religion, and were zealous in making converts to Christ. The new movement, inspired of God, spread rapidly from place to place. It is a sound assumption that the movement would have spread all over western Europe had it not been checked and frustrated by a cruel and relentless persecution. As it was, these unordained men, banded together in Christian love and fellowship, launched a spiritual revival that was revolutionary in its effects upon the lives of multiplied thousands. It was a real refreshing from the presence of the Lord.

The Waldenses were fiercely persecuted. They were treacherously attacked and shamefully mistreated. Thousands of them were exterminated in the most cruel manner. The Church and the state united to crush the sect and to destroy its members. The remnant was expelled from France and was compelled to find refuge in other countries. For the most part the Waldenses became amalgamated with other groups and lost their identity.

It is worthy of note that the principles of the Reformation so successfully supported by Luther were the same principles championed by Waldo and his followers three hundred years before Luther.

> *"Truth crushed to earth will rise again,*
> *The eternal years of God are hers."*

CHAPTER VII

JOHN WYCLIF AND REVIVALISM

In the fourteenth century there was a revival of historical importance in England under the inspiring leadership of John Wyclif. This revival was a continuation of the work of Pierre Waldo in the twelfth century and in several ways it moved in the same channel and carried forward the same emphases.

After Wyclif received his doctor's degree at Oxford University, he devoted himself to the learning of the age, the study of the Bible, and other intellectual and spiritual pursuits. He was recognized as a pre-eminent scholar and a devout Christian. After a long period of obscurity, he was made Master of Balliol College in Oxford, where he was known as the "Evangelical Doctor" and where he molded many choice minds.

He lost his position at the college because of his repeated attacks upon the Roman Church. He unsparingly denounced its sacerdotal pretensions and obvious corruptions, and he reached the conclusion that the Pope was antichrist, since his deeds were opposed to those of Christ. Wyclif was twice summoned before Church tribunals to answer for his attacks on the Church, but the nation defended and protected him. He steadfastly believed that the truth, having superior power, would conquer.

Wyclif translated the whole Bible into the language of the people, and he is called the father of our English Bible. He is recognized, also, as the founder of English prose writing.

He trained itinerant preachers and sent them out over England to evangelize and to make "Christ's law" known. Many of his former students at Oxford were recruited for the work. At first these preachers were called "poor priests," and they preached Christ all over England. Later these lay preachers were called "Lollards" in derision because they sang praises to the God of their salvation. They held fast to the Bible as the source of religious truth, and they could not be turned away from their holy mission by ugly threats of persecution and death.

Wyclif and his lay helpers were branded as heretics and severely persecuted. Some of them were executed. But in spite of the severe measures taken against them, they continued their evangelistic activities underground until revival fires were lighted over large areas of England. The good work which began under Waldo in France and Italy during the twelfth century, and under Wyclif in England in the fourteenth century, came to full fruition in Luther's Reformation in the sixteenth century.

Several teachers of Oxford lost their positions because of their loyalty to Wyclif, and when driven out of their own country, they fled to Germany. The divine spark which had been kindled within them was carried to Bohemia where they fled. John Huss, the eminent Bohemian reformer, at first regarded Wyclif and his work with disapproval; but after careful study of the Scriptures, he accepted the viewpoint of the English reformer and became the able leader of the evangelical movement in his own country.

Huss criticized the clergy because of the scandalous

manner of their lives and the gross corruptions of their practices. His fearless denunciation of sin and bold witness for Christ cost him his life. He was summoned to Rome but declined to obey the summons. Later he appeared before a council which was held at Constance after the emperor provided him with a safe conduct. He was arrested upon his arrival in the city and thrown into a dungeon, where he remained in chains for a year, after which he was given a speedy trial. He was offered the alternative of recantation or death. He chose death rather than a denial of truth, and on his forty-second birthday he was burned at the stake, after which his ashes were cast into the Rhine river. Judged by the canons of laws then prevailing his death was regarded as "judicial murder." Because the emperor violated the safe conduct promised Huss, a civil war broke out in Bohemia which lasted for twenty two years. This war against the emporer waged by those who followed the martyr's doctrine is known in history as the Hussite War.

John Wyclif escaped imprisonment and a violent death at the hands of those who opposed him; but forty four years after he died a natural death, his bones were burned, at the order of Rome, and his ashes were cast into the Avon river.

> *"The Avon to the Severn runs,*
> *The Severn to the sea,*
> *And Wyclif's dust shall spread abroad*
> *Wide as the waters be."*

The influence of Wyclif's character and reform work, especially of his English Bible, knows no limit of time or country.

We cannot adequately measure the full extent of our indebtedness to Pierre Waldo, John Wyclif, John Huss, and other reformers, before Luther's Reformation. They kept the Christian faith and the teachings of Christ alive in the world. Humanly considered, it is possible that without them, or others of like moral and spiritual caliber, pure and undefiled religion would have perished from the earth.

CHAPTER VIII

LUTHER'S REFORMATION

In the early part of the sixteenth century there was a mighty resurgence of Christian faith in Germany. This spiritual upheaval with its astounding vitality, was led by Martin Luther. This Reformation, as it was called, did not suddenly fall out of the sky. Rather, it was carried forward through many stormy years by brave men who prized truth and conscience, and honest conviction, above every other consideration.

Luther's Reformation marked the continuation and expansion of the reforms initiated by the Waldenses in France and Italy, the Lollards in England, and the Hussites in Germany. All groups stimulated interest in reading the Scriptures, protested against the many evils in the Roman Church, and vigorously professed a positive faith in the teachings of the holy Scriptures. Luther was supported in his reform work by a backlog of reserve strength and a reservoir of supporting good will scattered over western and central Europe. This accumulation of moral conviction and spiritual force established for Luther a wide base of operation. Furthermore, his spectacular success was made possible by the new translations of the Bible by William Tyndale and Miles Coverdale, and the invention of the printing press.

Prevailing conditions were favorable to the success of the Reformation. The people were shocked by the behavior of their popes. It was claimed that for sixty years before the Reformation, there had been only one

59

pope, "who could be called even a decent Christian." The revival of learning enabled thoughtful men to see the errors and abuses that existed within the Church. And, the people who had been shackled so long by a sense of corporate membership in the Church and the perfunctory discharge of external duties, were ready for personal religion and individual responsibility.

Luther was born in Saxony in the latter part of the fifteenth century. His humble parents gave him a strictly religious training. At eighteen years of age he entered the University of Erfurt. He began as a student of law, but later gave up this study and became a monk. Two years later he was ordained a priest and celebrated his first mass. The next year he was invited to teach moral philosophy at the University of Wittenberg, and a year later he became a teacher of theology. He discovered during his studies for class room work the key to his future theology—"The just shall live by faith." This truth became the key note of the Reformation. He knew that this doctrine was not in harmony with the accepted doctrines of his Church, but he highly resolved to follow the light of the Scriptures, whatever the consequences might be.

On October 31, 1517, Luther posted his Ninety-five Theses on the door of Castle Church in Wittenberg, Germany, with the intention of provoking a discussion of the issues he raised. But instead of prompting a frank debate, his action generated a storm that rocked the Roman Catholic Church to its foundations.

Luther was strongly opposed to the traffic in indulgencies which was practiced by the Church and which he believed was destroying the honor of the Church. In his

"95 Theses" he focused attention on this flagrant evil, and requested that it be corrected.

The two chief doctrines of the Reformation are well known: salvation alone by a single act of faith in the divine mercy and the sole and supreme authority of the Scriptures. "Man's sins can be forgiven only by grace through faith in Christ." The destructive force that works within us can be removed only by the grace of God. Luther's conscience was taken captive by God's Word. He was held fast by the Scriptures whose authority he placed above popes and councils.

The times were ripe for the reforms advocated by Luther, but the Church vigorously opposed him. The opposition was so sudden and merciless that it brought from Luther an outburst of righteous indignation. He was called, "God's angry man."

In spite of opposition Luther's efforts to correct evil conditions succeeded from the beginning. Within four years he had won the entire faculty of the University of Wittenberg to his doctrinal viewpoint. The students accepted the new teaching and the university became a training ground for the future leaders of the Reformation. Business men and monks, princes, knights, and scholars, rallied to Luther's defense.

The scholarly Philip Melanchthon came forward to write the theology of the Reformation. And the press gave it adequate publicity. John Calvin of Geneva and Ulrich Zwingli, the Swiss priest-reformer, gave Luther valuable help and encouragement. The people quickly rallied, and became articulate and active in their support of the new movement.

The Reformation, led by Luther, marked the rise of

Protestantism, which drew away from the Roman Catholic Church nearly all of the peoples of the Germanic race, and the entire Scandinavian population. And, it led to the establishment of a regenerated and reformed Church of Christ, which has several divisions, and which has extended its healing ministry to all parts of the world.

The Reformation emphasized the freedom of faith and the right of the individual to worship God in the way dictated by his private conscience. As a result divisive trends became manifest and denominational groups appeared. Someone has observed that "Protestantism is like an orchard of many different fruit trees, all of them good all of them growing, all of them bearing fruit."

Because of different doctrinal views stoutly held and stubbornly defended by the several Protestant groups that emerged, bitter controversy became prevalent, and the early Protestant churches did not project a foreign missionary program. History teaches that a thorough going revival stimulates renewed interest in missions, and it is regrettable that Protestantism in the early years of its existence did not initiate a vigorous missionary program. The missionary impulse was smothered by doctrinal controversy.

When Luther moved to correct the abuses that were corrupting and destroying the influence of the Church, he had no intention of breaking with its fellowship and leading a religious and social revolution. But several years after he nailed up his Ninety-five Theses he decided that the break with Rome was inevitable. The leaders of the Church regarded him as a heretic and a betrayer of religion. He repeatedly expressed his willingness to be convinced of his error on the basis of the Scriptures.

But when those who opposed him found themselves unable to do this, they determined to silence him or destroy him.

Shortly after the die was cast and the issues sharply drawn, the pope acted swiftly, and Luther was excommunicated. But Luther could not be silenced by this drastic action. When the pope's Bull of excommunication reached him, he reacted with haughty defiance, and publicly burned the document.

Four years after Luther posted his Ninety-five Theses he was summoned before the Imperial Diet at Worms. The Diet demanded that he renounce his writings and surrender his convictions. But he, with reckless abandon, told the Diet that he would not surrender his convictions or conscience to any power on earth unless convinced by the word of God, or evident reason, of his error. "Here I stand; I cannot do otherwise; so help me God!"

There is brought before us here one of the supreme scenes of human history. Jesus standing unperturbed before Pontius Pilate; Paul boldly standing before King Agrippa; and Luther fearlessly standing before the Diet at Worms, are scenes worthy of everlasting remembrance.

The Diet declared Luther a public outlaw, and as he had already been excommunicated by the Church, there was nothing more his enemies could do except take his life. This they planned to do, but loyal friends concealed him at Wartburg, and their evil plans were frustrated. During the period of his concealment at Wartburg, he translated the New Testament. After the storm subsided, he returned to Wittenburg and resumed his work at the university. Thanks to a protecting Providence he never suffered the slightest injury. "He lived triumphantly until his work was finished and passed away peacefully in the presence of his friends with loud thanksgiving to God."

Luther's Reformation, with both spiritual and political overtones, was the most significant event in the world since the days of the apostles. Without this purifying awakening the Church, as it was known at the time, might have been cast out and trodden under the feet of men. The Reformation sounded the death-knell of ecclesiastical and political tyranny over the souls, and minds, and lives, of men.

Lyman Abbott declared that "humanity is always needing an operation for spiritual cataract." This truth applies to the Christian Church. When the Church loses its sense of mission and its passion for the souls of lost men, it needs to be revived and re-vitalized. When the Church becomes unclean in its life, it needs revival fires to cleanse and purify it. There come times in the life of the church when its salvation lies in a visitation from on high, a spiritual refreshing from the presence of the Lord. The Church in the early part of the sixteenth century had reached such a low level of spiritual life as to require drastic spiritual surgery, and God called Martin Luther to do the work that needed to be done. He left the statement that God had led him in the work he did.

History has assigned Luther a niche which will always be his. His stature grows with the passing of the centuries. No man since Paul has been so signally honored and widely praised. Even Catholic historians accord him due praise, and recognize him as the man of his age. "The ovation to his memory on the four hundredth anniversary of his birth surpassed in enthusiasm anything that has ever been rendered to the memory of a mortal man."

Luther abides as a massive figure, a transcendent personality, and a mighty Gibraltar of spiritual strength.

CHAPTER IX

THE WESLEYAN REVIVAL

This chapter will deal with the Wesleyan revival which occurred in England during the eighteenth century. It will be considered from the standpoint of the spiritual re-birth of a nation rather than from the standpoint of the origin and development of a significant denomination. Careful students claim that the Methodist Church which arose out of the revival represents only a small part of its accomplishment, and when we fully understand the total effects of the revival upon the life of England, we are ready to accept this claim.

It was not the intention of Luther, when he attempted to reform a corrupt Church, to leave the church of his fathers and start other churches; neither did Wesley intend to leave the established Church of England when he led the effort to revive its fading life. But the Roman Church excommunicated Luther and the Church of England closed its doors against Mr. Wesley and the lay preachers whom he trained for evangelistic service. "A year before his death Mr. Wesley expressed the fear that "when the Methodists leave the established church God will leave them."

When the Jewish religion lost its ability to provide adequate food for the souls of men, many Jews became disciples of Jesus and supported the redemptive movement which he launched. For the same reason members of the Roman and Anglican churches left their churches and became identified with the spiritual movements started by Luther and Wesley.

66

It was the worthy purpose of these leaders to restore the principles of primitive Christianity. This could not be done without a re-discovery of the ancient gospel which church leaders had lost somewhere along the way. When they discovered God's redemptive message in Christ and experienced it in their own hearts, and began to teach and preach it, they provoked conflict which led to cleavage, and these great scholars and able Christian leaders were repudiated by their respective churches. Mr. Wesley continued as a clergyman of the Church of England to the close of his earthly life, but his great work of reviving religion and saving the nation was carried on outside the church and without encouragement from its leaders.

Doctor T. R. Glover, a distinguished Baptist minister, ranks John Wesley with Paul, Augustine, and Luther. He deserves praise and honor from all who compose the Christian fellowship, irrespective of denominational affiliation. He belongs to Christendom. His influence has reached all continents of the earth. England, which during the first ten years of his redemptive work poured contempt and abuse upon him, came to respect him, and conferred upon him honors reserved for their most illustrious sons. He was accorded a place in Westminster Abbey, England's Hall of Fame, and Oxford University, where he was so cruelly jeered during his student years, honored him by the display of his bust and portrait.

As the University of Wittenberg was the spring-board of the Reformation, the University of Oxford was the starting point of the Wesleyan revival, and the place where many of its leaders were trained. It is apparent that spiritual revivals are not only needed in the back-woods and on the frontiers of civilization; but they are also needed in seats of higher learning, and may prove as successful in such settings as in any other place.

According to Mr. Wesley the revival with which he was associated had its origin at Oxford University in 1729 when several young men met together for prayer and the study of the Scriptures. These young men were called "Methodists" in derision because of their methodical religious ways, even as the disciples of Christ were first called "Christians" in a taunting spirit by the heathen population of Syrian Antioch.

There is sufficient reason for believing that the Wesleyan revival began when Mr. Wesley had his heart warming experience at Aldersgate in 1739. He was thirty-five years of age when he had his "evangelical conversion" experience. He had been a clergyman in the Church of England for several years before Aldersgate, but he did not have a vital gospel message for the people. After his conversion experience he wrote in his Journal, "I gave the people Christ." He and his Oxford companions in labor, and thousands of lay preachers whom he trained, went out among the people of England, and wherever they traveled they gave the people Christ. It was the message that England needed, and the only message that has proved effective in producing a spiritual awakening since Christ died upon a cross.

Mr. Wesley began his revival work at an hour when England must decide between a revival of religion and a return to God, and a political revolution. There was no other alternative. There were two open roads, one led to Christ and a spiritual re-birth of the nation, and the other led toward the vortex of a bloody revolution.

When Mr. Wesley came on the scene, with Christ in

his heart and by his side, England "was in the grips of an Ice Age, better known in history as the Age of Reason. Many regarded not only the organized church, but the Christian way of life, as dead." Many believed that the religion of Christ was an invention of the imagination and the discussion of religion in polite society was frowned upon. The clergymen had lost sight of a redeeming Christ and had no saving message for lost men. The Church as a redemptive community no longer existed. It no longer offered an uplifted Christ to draw the people to the Church and lift them into a more wholesome way of life. The Church was dead, and the religion of Christ had for the most part faded from the life of the nation.

The moral life of England had reached an unprecedented low. Many prominent statesmen were distinguished by grossness of conduct, and the masses of the people lost aii sense of moral decency and social responsibility. England was without hope and without God and was fast moving toward the destruction ever in store for nations that forget God. Isaiah spoke words to his generation that might have been spoken to eighteenth century England:

> "The whole head is sick,
> And the whole heart faint.
> From the sole of the foot even to
> the head,
> There is no soundness in it,
> But bruises and sores
> And bleeding wounds."

It was during these dark days and troublous times that a spiritual dawn appeared over England. The Church of England was revived and a new missionary impulse was born. Mr. Wesley was fittingly called "the horseman of the Lord," as Francis Asbury was later called "the prophet of the long road." After the churches were closed to Mr. Wesley and his local preachers, they carried the gospel message to people on the streets and in the open fields, to the tinners of Cornwall and the miners of Kingswood, and to the shopkeepers and factory workers.

Christ was brought near to the lost and neglected. Mr. Wesley won and held the respect of men who earned their daily bread by the toil of their hands and the sweat of their brows. Many of the local preachers were recruited from their ranks. A sound labor party emerged, which later became the Labor Party and at times the ruling party of the nation. Because of the religious influence of this "party" England was not drawn into the bloody revolution which a few years later convulsed France.

A clear retrospective view of history confirms our belief that Mr. Wesley, under God, gloriously succeeded in accomplishing the work he undertook. He restored the ancient gospel, rekindled a spirit of piety within the Church of England, and revived the dying religion of his day. His evangelistic labors were extensive. The long circuit he traveled extended from London to Bristol, to New Castle on the Tyne river, and down to London. During the fifty odd years of his labors, he traveled this circuit seventy-five times. Furthermore, he made other evangelistic tours. He visited Ireland twenty-one times, Scotland twenty times, and Wales twenty-four times. The influence of his revival movement has reached all parts of the globe. It started more than two hundred years ago, and it has not yet run its course. It produced the largest Protestant denomination in the world, with a membership, counting adherents, near the thirty million mark. The vitality of the movement is still in evidence on every front of the world where the work of Christ is carried forward.

What the Wesleyan revival accomplished under adverse conditions should convince us beyond a shadow of doubt that men dedicated to the purpose of God and clothed with divine power can promote spiritual revivals whenever and wherever needed.

CHAPTER X

AMERICAN REVIVALS AND EVANGELISTS

The early Christian Church was impelled onward over the Mediterranean world by repeated Pentecosts, and fresh outpourings of the Holy Spirit. It was the presence of Christ operating through the Holy Spirit that kept the church vital and on the march. We find here the secret of the strength and progress of the Christian Church ever since.

Spiritual revivals have played a significant part in the history of our counrty, contributing much to her moral strength and spiritual power. During crucial periods of our history there have come spiritual refreshings upon our people which have molded their character and established spiritual trends without which our national destiny would not have been shaped as it was.

In this connection it should be observed with particular care that the term "revival" represents only one of the several facets of evangelism. It does not exclude any other method of evangelism. Jesus practiced what is called personal evangelism. St. John in his Gospel records thirteen examples of Jesus dealing with individuals. In the New Testament there are many evidences of personal soul-winning. When a person becomes imbued with the spirit and ideals of Christ, there is the impulse to tell others the story of redeeming love.

Many churches today carry on a permanent program of evangelism with lay teams calling on prospective members. This organization is called "The Fisherman's Club," and it may operate effectively in both city and country situations. This method of winning the unsaved and dislocated is responsible for adding many members to the churches.

The life of the church has been enriched by pastor-evangelists, such as C. H. Spurgeon, George W. Truett, Charles L. Goodell, and many others. In the published sermons of Phillips Brooks and Charles H. Spurgeon about half are evangelistic and half pastoral.

Mass evangelism, or the revival method, has always had a prominent place in the Church of Christ. The National Council of Churches has extensive plans for its use. As mass industry has been perfected and universally accepted to the great benefit of mankind, it would certainly contradict and run counter to the spirit of the present age if the church should lessen in the least its emphasis on mass evangelism.

In a consideration of the benefits of revivals, the fact that the law of ebb and flow is operating must be taken into account. Spiritual resurgence is usually followed by a recession. When a spiritual tide reaches its crest, it is often followed by spiritual decline and indifference. This has been palpably true in the religious life of our country. High tides of spiritual interest and power have been broken as they beat against the rocks of unbelief and wickedness. But this does not imply that a revival is useless and a waste of time and energy. The history of revivals as related to the Church and the welfare of our republic emphasizes the paramount importance of spiritual revivals.

In this chapter, "American Revivals and Evangelists" will be discussed; but it should be stated at the outset that only those revivals that have attracted wide attention, and only those evangelists who have stood out in popular thinking can be considered. I am aware that tens of thousands of effective revivals, in small churches and limited areas, have been conducted throughout our land and whose total impact upon our life cannot be fully measured. I am, also, aware that a host of lesser evangelists have revived dead churches, and won multiplied thousands to Christ. These useful evangelists may not have received popular acclaim, but we may feel assured that their names are written in the Lamb's Book of Life.

A

THE GREAT AWAKENING, 1733-1744.

The two human agents of the Great Awakening were Jonathan Edwards and George Whitefield. It began in a quiet congregational rural parish, in Northampton, Massachusetts, where the scholarly Doctor Edwards was minister. A small group of young people called upon their minister and talked with him about their need, and the community's need, of God, after which the minister began to preach dynamic gospel sermons that stirred the hearts and conscience of all who heard him. He at once gained a reputation as a preacher of commanding influence, and the whole community was spiritually quickened. Within six months three hundred persons were converted and added to the church.

There was scarcely a person in the community, old or young, who was left unconcerned about the things of eternity. Sinners repented and turned from darkness to the light, and from their life of sin unto God. Songs of joy and thanksgiving to God were heard on every side.

A revival like this could not be confined to a small parish of a thousand souls. It spread like a conflagration to all parts of the state, and within a short time its in-influence was felt in several other states.

After three years of intense spiritual interest and fervent activity, there was a gradual decrease of interest which continued until 1739 when the second phase of the Great Awakening began. This was led by the English evangelist George Whitefield, who later assisted in the launching of the Wesleyan revival in England. He was widely known as an eloquent pulpit orator, and huge crowds gathered to hear him wherever he preached.

Whitefield united with Samuel Blair and Gilbert Ter-rent in evangelistic labors. These two men had been as-sociated with Edwards in the first phase of the revival, and they knew that there was still much work to be done. Whitefield, Blair, and Terrent made an effective team, and they conducted successful revivals in New York City, and Boston and other centers of large populations. They spent eighteen months in the New England States, and it was estimated that they won fifty thousand souls to Christ. The churches of the entire area were revived and shared the fruits of the great awakening.

At the close of the campaign in New York and New England, Whitefield and his co-workers moved on to Vir-ginia and other southern colonies, and wherever they went revival fires were kindled, churches devoid of spiritual life were awakened, and thousands were led to Christ.

The Great Awakening which began under the leader-ship of Jonathan Edwards and was carried forward by Whitefield and many others, continued in some form or other until the beginning of the Revolutionary War. Many new churches were organized and several colleges established. This historical revival united the people spiritually and prepared the way for the political union of the disunited colonies, which proved a vital and decisive factor in winning the war for independence and founding our Republic.

B

THE GREAT REVIVAL—1800

This revival of cardinal importance to our national life had two bases of operation, one in the West and the other in the East. In the West the revival represented an effort to save the American frontier from a growing wickedness that threatened to blot out Christian civilization. In the East the revival directed its attack against a French brand of infidelity which had gained a strong foothold in schools of higher education, and threatened the destruction of the Christian faith.

In the West the revival first appeared in Tennessee, but it soon spread into Kentucky where it reached its crest. The revival was promoted by leaders of different denominations working together. The frontier camp-meeting came into existence during this period and was widely and successfully used during the following years.

In the year 1801 the revival of the West reached spectacular manifestations at Cane Ridge Presbyterian Church in Bourbon County, Kentucky. The services lasted for several days, and at times continued throughout the night. The church was crowded beyond its capacity and the throngs flowed into the woods surrounding the church.

Several services were conducted on the grounds at the same time. The divine power was manifested in the conviction and conversion of sinners.

Multitudes gathered at Cane Ridge not only from Kentucky, but from Ohio, and Tennessee, as well. Distinguished men from all walks of life were there. The governor of Kentucky, editors, judges, politicians, and leading business men, came to behold the mighty works of God. The roads were crowded with carriages, horsemen, and footmen. About thirty thousand people gravitated toward the place where God was manifesting his redeeming grace.

The Cane Ridge revival was expanded to many places in other states. Those present diffused the revival spirit in their respective communities, and the heavenly flame spread in all directions. Thosuands of souls were saved, and the rising tide of iniquity was checked.

It is not possible to catalogue fully the results of a revival because many of the results are intangible. But certain definite results of the revival in the West have been recorded and are well known. Ten thousand members were added to the churches in Kentucky, and the Church of Christ entered upon a new era of progress. The denomination of the "Disciples of Christ" emerged out of the revival, and it has become one of the major divisions of the church of Christ in our country.

Some of the revivals of the past have had highly emotional overtones, and have been characterized by dramatic tableau. This was true during the early stages of the Wesleyan revival in England, and it was, also, true of some of the revivals during the pioneer period of our country.

The unusual manifestations and the strange agitations that occurred at Cane Ridge, I do not understand and shall not attempt to explain. It is worthy of note that the revival in the East which appeared at the same time, was not accompanied by unusual excitement and bizarre behavior.

As previously stated the Great Revival of the period under discussion had a double base, one in the West and the other in the East. Timothy Dwight who served as a chaplain in the Revolutionary War, and wrote the much beloved hymn, "I Love Thy Kingdom, Lord," became president of Yale College in 1795. He soon discovered that the college was honeycombed with infidelity. The students were blatantly articulate in their unbelief. In signing their signatures they often wrote "infidel" after their names as a gesture of pride and defiance.

The new president did not in any way interfere with the freedom of his students. Rather he encouraged them to list the reasons for their unbelief. After listening patiently to the expression of their doubts, he gave a series of chapel talks that dealt with the questions they had raised and the arguments they had made. As a result of these chapel sermons, a marked change became manifest among the students. There came upon the college community a visitation from on high. More than a third of the students were converted, and half of this number entered the gospel ministry. Drunkenness, gambling, and profanity disappeared from campus life, and infidelity was driven from the hearts and minds of the college family, and became a vanishing force in the history of the new republic.

Following the established pattern of other revivals, the interest tapered off and partially subsided. But this was followed by a resurgence of spiritual interest in the college and the results were more sweeping than the first. It is said that there were seekers of God in every room on the campus. The revival fires spread to Dartmouth and Princeton and other schools.

A spiritual upheaval of such intensity and large proportions could not be confined in a few schools. Its influence spread throughout New England, New York, Pennsylvania, and Ohio. Consequently, the revivals of the West and the East became united, and proved a mighty force in forming the national character.

When this Great Revival began on two fronts at the turn of the century, only one sixth of the people were members of the churches, the moral conditions were distressingly bad, and a brazen infidelity was gaining ground. These unsavory conditions were changed for the better within a period of a few years. The churches over an extensive area were quickened into newness of life, and the religion of Christ became dominant in the affairs of men.

A short time before, our war for freedom had been won, and a constitutional form of government set up. Freedom as we understand it, is a religious concept and cannot be maintained without divine assistance. The Great Revival, practically considered, reached the entire nation and gave the people a fuller understanding of the freedom they had achieved and prepared them in heart and mind to carry forward their new government enterprises. As the Great Awakening prepared our people for the Revolutionary struggle, the Great Revival qualified them to make secure the fruits of their victorious revolutionary struggle.

The Great Revival followed the New Testament pattern. It was produced by the preaching of the word of God and by importunate prayer. It inspired a comprehensive interest in furthering the cause of Christ. Theological seminaries were founded, the American Bible Society was organized, and missionary societies were established. Truly, this was a revival sent from God for the saving of souls, and the healing of the nation.

C

EVANGELISTS:

CHARLES G. FINNEY

Mr. Finney practiced law until the time of his conversion in 1821. Three years after his spiritual awakening he was licensed to preach, and began his evangelistic activity, which line of work he faithfully followed until 1860, when the infirmities of age compelled him to retire. He conducted successful revivals in America and England and won tens of thousands to Christ. His "Lectures on Revivals" is one of the best books ever published on mass evangelism. When I served as minister of churches, it was my practice to read this book before revival efforts were undertaken in the churches I served.

Doctor Finney served as minister of churches, and as professor of theology at Oberlin College, of which school he was subsequently president; but none of these duties prevented his evangelistic activity. In his preaching his appeals were directed at the conscience rather than the emotions; but the feelings he aroused were so intense and the demonstrations in his revivals so unusual, that his revival work provoked much criticism and opposition.

MOODY AND SANKEY

Mr. Moody was converted in 1855 while working as a salesman in a Boston shoe store, after which he engaged in missionary work in Chicago. He started and taught a non-affiliated Sunday School class, which was later organized into a church of which he became the lay pastor.

One day, as he was walking along the streets of New York City, he had a spiritual experience known in the early Christian Church as the baptism of the Holy Spirit. According to his testimony this new experience clothed him with divine power and made his preaching effective in reaching the unsaved. His life was now dedicated fully to God and wholly given to His service.

In 1870 the Moody-Sankey evangelistic team was formed: Moody the preacher, and Sankey the singer. Two years later they conducted revival services in London, England, and thousands accepted Christ. In this revival a young doctor with skeptical leanings, was converted, who a short time later went to Labrador, as a medical missionary, where he spent the rest of his life. Sir Wilfred Thomason Grenfell is affectionately remembered as "The Labrador Doctor."

After Moody and Sankey returned home from London, invitations to conduct revivals came to them from many cities. They led revival efforts in Brooklyn, New York City, Chicago, Boston, Baltimore, St. Louis, Kansas City, and other large cities, and wherever they went their revivals produced high tides of evangelistic fervor and demonstrations of divine power. They carried their gospel message, and the divine spark, to smaller cities across the land. They visited the Pacific Coast and conducted short services in several cities where they organized and inspired many evangelists and workers who carried forward the good work.

During the Chicago Fair in 1893 Moody seized the opportunity to preach Christ to the throngs that visited the fair. Churches and other buildings near the fair grounds were used for the services. Open air services were held, and on Sundays Moody preached in a large circus tent which held ten thousand people. This unusual campaign resulted in thousands of conversions.

Because the multitudes that desired to hear Mr. Moody preach and Mr. Sankey sing, could not be accomodated, it became necessary to build large tabernacles. These were filled to capacity.

These evangelists reached several million people with their message, and their converts have been estimated at a half million. The impact of their labors was felt all over the nation.

Doctor Henry Drummond declared that Moody was the greatest man produced during his century. Many distinguished evangelists have appeared during the history of our country, and Mr. Moody is as widely and favorably known as any other who has labored among us.

SUNDAY AND RODEHEAVER

"Billy" Sunday was born in a log cabin and reared in an orphanage. He won nation-wide fame as a major league baseball star before his conversion and spectacular evangelistic activities. He began his religious work by serving as promotional assistant to Evangelist J. Wilbur Chapman. When Mr. Chapman left the evangelistic field and returned to the pastorate in 1896, Sunday launched out on his own as an evangelist.

Homer Rodeheaver who passed to his eternal reward on December 18, 1955, was Sunday's team-mate, and musical director for twenty years. He traveled across the country and over the world with Sunday on evangelistic campaigns. They conducted gigantic campaigns in New York City, Philadelphia, Boston, Cleveland, Detroit, Indianapolis, Chicago, Cincinnati, and many other large cities. It is claimed that he preached to a million people, and that through his influence thousands traveled the "saw dust trail" to God.

Mr. Sunday was the most sensational evangelist that has ever appeared among us. It was my privilege to hear him several times, and I shall never forget his contorted brow, his flaying arms, and flowing perspiration. He was highly dramatic and deeply stirred those who heard him. His work gave mass evangelism a much needed boost and inspired revival efforts throughout the country.

Sunday and his efforts were endorsed by John D. Rockefeller and other prominent business men. A large majority of our Protestant ministers gave Mr. Sunday their approval and active support. Conversely, he had many vigorous critics who condemned his methods and declared that his work was superficial and would not abide. Dean Andrew West of Princeton, denied him permission to speak on the campus "in the name of purity and sanctity of our Christian faith."

One biographer states that Mr. Sunday's cyclonic influence waned during the "roaring twenties." The economic depression struck in the early thirties, and other effective evangelists appeared on the scene. Mr. Sunday was most effective between 1910 and 1920. "He died in 1935, most forgotten of men."

HENRY C. MORRISON

After the Honorable William Jennings Bryan listened to a sermon by Doctor Morrison, he pronounced him the greatest pulpit orator in America. He served as college president, and editor of a religious journal, and during his last years, founded a theological seminary, and was its president and guiding influence to the close of his earthly life.

Like Charles G. Finney, Doctor Morrison did not allow other heavy duties to interfere with his evangelistic work. He conducted great revivals all over the country. He would respond to a call to a small church as readily as he would to a large one. The influence of this man fully dedicated to the will of God is felt today in thousands of places throughout our land, and in other parts of the world as well. He was the recognized leader of evangelistic forces over a period of fifty odd years and won ten thousand souls to Christ. He gave a rugged emphasis to revivalism at a time when the temper of the churches was uncongenial to his convictions and efforts. But he never wavered in his defense of the revival concept. He believed that a revival of spiritual religion would provide a solution for most of the ills that afflict mankind.

Doctor Morrison was at his best when preaching to preachers. Preachers respected and loved him, and he inspired them to greater efforts in the work of the Lord. He kindled revival fires in their hearts, and they went from his presence to exalt Christ and to spread scriptural holiness over the land.

A host of lesser known evangelists, not discussed in this chapter, have rendered yeoman service in bringing the lost to Christ and building the soul of America. A list of nationally known evangelists would not be complete without the names of Sam P. Jones, R. A. Torrey, J. Wilbur Chapman, S. D. Gordon, and many others. "Gipsy" Smith of England promoted several successful revivals in our country.

The next chapter will be given to a discussion of Evangelist Billy Graham and his extensive and successful revival activities.

CHAPTER XI

EVANGELIST BILLY GRAHAM

William Franklin Graham was born at Charlotte, North Carolina, November 7, 1918, and at thirty-seven years of age is one of our most widely and favorably known evangelists. The latest religious encyclopedia published gives comparatively large space to the life and work of Mr. Graham. Such high recognition of one so young and whose work is far from finished, is unusual and arresting.

It has not been my privilege to know Mr. Graham in a personal way, nor is our denominational affiliation the same, but I have avidly followed his meteoric career with increasing interest and appreciation. I have listened to several of his weekly radio sermons, which are carried by nine hundred stations, and heard all over the world; I read his daily syndicated column, My Answer, and I have followed his revival campaigns as they have been reported through various media of publicity. Like Luther during the Reformation, Mr. Graham has received from the public press full coverage of his revival work, the warmest praise, and the strongest support.

After Mr. Graham preached to thirty thousand people in Geneva, Switzerland, which resulted in a thousand decisions for Christ, a Roman Catholic newspaper observed, "It is up to Catholics to live their faith integrally, and rediscover that spirit of conquest and dynamic qualities of the early Christians. If Billy Graham by his own dynamic qualities was able to make Catholics understand this, the message he brought to Geneva will not have been in vain."

Mr. Graham is universally recognized as a pivotal figure of his generation. To him belongs the accolade of greatness in the sight of the Lord. It may be said of him as it was said of John the Baptist, he is "a man sent from God." Not only do the "common people" hear him gladly, but distinguished scholars and heads of state as well. He has displayed a terrific ability to reach the masses, and, also, churchmen, educators, statesmen, and men of affairs in all walks of life. When he was in London the Queen of England and the Archbishop of Canterbury received him with the greatest cordiality and heard his dynamic gospel message with undisguised approval. It should be emphasized in this connection that favorable publicity and universal adulation have not obscured his vision nor warped his perspective. He remains a man of deep humility and unquestioned sincerity.

Mr. Graham is a denominationalist and is proud of his particular division of the Church; but he has a sense of that which is vital in religion, and places the salvation of souls above all other considerations. He has the capacity to lead all denominations in a united revival effort to reach and save the lost. His object is not to build up one particular denomination, but to make converts to Christ and to make the Church of Christ strong in all of its divisions. There will not develop from his momentous work a new division of the Church as resulted from the work of Luther and Wesley, as he will not be denied the fellowship of the church of his childhood as Luther and Wesley were.

Billy Graham was converted when seventeen years

of age, and after receiving a college degree and doing graduate work, he was ordained a Baptist minister and was one of its foremost leaders. Later he founded the Billy Graham Evangelistic Association with headquarters at Minneapolis, and dedicated his life to full-time evangelistic service. He soon rose to national prominence. His revival campaigns across the nation turned the thoughts of men back to God.

During his Los Angeles campaign huge crowds attended the services. Many were converted including several of the outstanding "stars" of Hollywood. He has conducted successful revivals in Houston and Forth Worth, Texas; Columbia, South Carolina; Washington, D. C.; Memphis, Shreveport, Louisiana; Pittsburgh; Seattle, and other large cities. As a result of these well planned campaigns, millions heard his messages in the services and on the radio and thousand acknowledged Christ as Savior and Lord.

Mr. Graham went to London, England in 1954 to lead a city wide revival effort. His stature already high was enhanced by the large success of this effort. The services, supported by prayer groups in London and over the world, continued for three months, and there were thirty thousand decisions for Christ.

Following the London campaign, Mr. Graham and his helpers launched a campaign in Glasgow, Scotland, and preached to about a half million people, and won twenty-three thousand more souls to Christ.

At the close of the London revival services a London

daily editorialized as follows: "It can truly be called the phenomenon of the mid-century. It may not be too much to hope that it may be the start of a spiritual renaissance." A British columnist wrote, "This is the ultimate spiritual energy that has always changed the world."

Mr. Graham visited continental Europe and preached to large audiences in several cities. Seventy-five thousand came to hear him in Berlin and about a third of them came from behind the Iron Curtain.

The marked success of Mr. Graham is not an accident. His services are saturated with the Scriptures; he depends upon the Holy Spirit for guidance and power; he has organized prayer groups all over the world who daily pray for him and his work; he enlists the support of all Protestant church groups; and, he has the unqualified backing of the secular and religious press.

Mr. Graham never attempts a city-wide revival without thorough preparation. In January he met with six hundred ministers, public officials, and civic leaders, in Louisville, Kentucky, to prepare them for the services to be held in that city in the fall of 1956. He said to these sponsors, "If this crusade does not affect your crime and divorce rate, I shall be disappointed. God is going to do something great for this great city."

The question has been raised as to the lasting effects of Mr. Graham's revivals. A careful investigation in London, a year after his work there, answers this important question. It was revealed that two-thirds of the converts had united with the churches and were faithful in life and service. This affords solid proof that the results achieved are genuine, and are more than an "expression of stupid emotionalism," as some have charged. The English clergymen and leaders of the press agree that the London revival brought about a mighty work of God among the people.

When Mr. Graham plans a city campaign, the newspaper fraternity is invited to participate in the planning. As a result full coverage and publicity are assured. Charles G. Finney did not believe it possible to have a revival covering an entire city unless the revival was made the dominant interest of the city. The daily papers can play a leading part in creating favorable conditions. When the churches of a city unite in a revival effort, the press will usually go the limit in supporting the enterprise.

Editors and reporters of the secular press are not interested in theological hair-splitting, and sectarian differences. The picture they see is an over-all one—the sermons preached, the interest shown, the size of the choir, the number attending, and the number of converts made. A spiritual awakening that stirs a city, vitally affects the lives of men in all of the areas of their being. Newspaper reporters are realistic in their appraisal of unusual events, and down to earth in their reporting. They know what real religion is, and they are impartially objective in reporting any spiritual phenomena that may appear in their city.

Billy Graham has spear-headed a revival movement whose influence has been deeply felt in all parts of his own country and in other parts of the world. He symbolizes mass evangelism and is its most vigorous and effective exponent. He has lifted revivalism into a prominence which it has had only a few times before during the entire history of the Christian Church. He has preached the vital gospel truth, with clear, firm faith, and the Church has been revitalized, and the Christian fellowship enlarged. Many who believe that Christ is the hope of the world have been nerved and strengthened to carry forward the Christian enterprise to a successful and triumphant conclusion.

Mr. Graham has fewer critics than most outstanding evangelists.. But he has drawn light criticism both in England and America. The criticisms heard are not directed at him personally. They have to do with his revival methods. But it may be truthfully said that these mild criticisms are completely invalidated by the course of events and the results registered.

Washington City is regarded by many as the capital of the world. In order to keep his fingers upon the religious life of the nation and of the world, Mr. Graham has moved his headquarters from Minneapolis to Washington. He is known and respected by many leaders of several nations, and his presence in Washington will prove a lasting benediction to many. Doubtless his influence in our nation's capital will tone up the moral fiber of the city and lift to higher levels the moral and spiritual life of the nation.

The splendid work of Mr. Graham inspired an editorial which appeared some time ago in the daily Lexington Herald, Lexington, Kentucky. This chapter will be closed by quoting an excerpt from this editorial:

"Much like the phenomena that followed upon the first preaching of the gospel, when the apostles performed miracles and turned the world upside down, the conversion of thousands and the deepening and enrichment of experience among great numbers, are in the line of tradition beginning at Pentecost."

CHAPTER XII

THE CURRENT REVIVAL

Unless the signs are false and the accumulated evidence misleading, we are in the midst of a large scale spiritual awakening in this country. The revival of religious interest began about fifteen years ago, and it has moved forward with increasing momentum until it has reached all areas of our national life. It is not believed that it has yet reached the summit of its strength and the fullness of its achievement.

Apart from God's special dealings with the Chosen People, the Scriptures teach that He is no respecter of races and nations, and it would be an unwarrantable presumption for us to claim that God has shown special favor to our nation. But this does not prevent our tracing God's providential dealings with us in some of the most critical periods of our national history. Spiritual refreshings have come upon our people when most needed. The current revival followed the most devastating economic debacle and spiritual black out in the history of our country. "We have witnessed a religious resurgence, a move back to God. The confusion and frustration of the twenties and thirties are being replaced by a robust faith."

Much credit is due our Christian leaders who kept faith and hope alive during the several years when spiritual religion had to fight for its life. Our leaders were caught in an upheaval of history that strained their faith to the breaking point; but they never wavered in their allegiance to Christ. The morals of the people reached a new low

93

and ethical values declined to the vanishing point, which was followed by an economic crash that rocked the nation; but our Christian leaders held fast to their faith in God, developed their strategy for major spiritual operations, and hopefully looked forward to better and brighter days.

The present day revival did not originate in any particular place, and it has not been typed and dominated by one dynamic personality. Billy Graham has done much to spread the revival, but the fires had been kindled before he appeared on the scene. He was sensitive to the signs of the times and as the revival fires burned on the altar of his heart, he felt that the hour had arrived to launch a mighty movement to conquer the soul of the world for Christ. Possibly, he had the conviction that God had called him to make a large contribution to the rising tide of revivalism. Be this as it may, we know for a certainty that Mr. Graham arrived on the revival scene preaching the gospel of the Savior and the resurrection faith of the early Church, and calling the multitudes to repentance and faith in God. He carried the evangel to several major cities of the nation, and the revival trend was greatly accelerated, leaped forward, and the river of salvation already flowing swiftly became a rushing torrent, broke from its channel, and flooded the entire country.

But the current revival does not bear the stamp of Mr. Graham nor of any other single person. Thousands of pastors, evangelists, and Christian workers, throughout the land, are responsible, under God, for the revival that is stirring our people. They have kindled revival fires on thousands of altars, and protested against a way of life that had no room for God and pleaded with the people to return to the God of their salvation.

It is the history of notable revivals to appear at certain definite places and then to mushroom. This was true of the "Great Awakening" and of the "Great Revival." But the current revival marks a departure from the established pattern, as it has had no particular center, and it has not been inspired and guided by a single recognized leader. Revivalism is on the march throughout the land and all divisions of the Church have been affected. The Roman Catholic Church, and those of the Jewish faith, and Protestant groups, are all manifesting a renewed interest in building up their fellowships. There is a contagious revival mood abroad in the land, and the total impact upon our people is revolutionary in its effect.

Our churches with the effective assistance of television and the radio have made us familiar with several inspiring slogans: Back to the Church Movement, Back to the Synagogue, Back to God, Youth for Christ, See You in Church, Give God a Chance, The Answer is God, and several other such slogans, which indicate that Christ is passing by. I heard enough gospel during the Christmas season on television and the radio to save the world. Our leaders in all departments of life seem to be aware that something unusual and supernatural is taking place among us.

The following quotation from a church paper tells of a revival effort in a single community: "A total of twelve hundred and thirty seven visits were made during the first week of the revival. There were eighty decisions for Christ and a hundred and forty two new members won. The first week of the revival was devoted to home visitation and cottage prayer-meetings, and preaching services were planned for the second week." If we multiply this effort by several thousand such efforts taking place all over the country, we will have a general idea of what is occurring. This is not a spasmodic revival, but a movement of God with a wide base and great depth of strength. Generally considered, the current revival "is of the people, by the people, for the people." It reaches from the nation's capital to the grass roots of American life. Never before in the history of our country was a revival so widely and highly praised, and ably supported.

We are passing through a period of deep spiritual hunger and earnest seeking after God. This is not an arbitrary assertion unsupported by visible evidence. There is as much substantial and convincing evidence to support this assertion as there is to support the claims of achievements that have taken place in other fields, during the same period.

Professor Toynbee says, "Religion has sprung up again in the human heart. There is a decided movement toward religion in the Western world. If there is no religious revival, the outlook for the West is unpromising." This clear statement from a man with an exceptional knowledge of history, must be regarded as highly significant. Arthur Strickland adds weight to the above statement when he observes that "history encourages the hope that society can again be redeemed through a spiritual awakening." In another connection Professor Toynbee develops the thesis that, "The breakdown of the established order is the occasion of the rise of a new religion or the rebirth of an old one."

Our Secretary of State, Mr. John Foster Dulles, says, "We need a spiritual revival that will give the people a sense of the purpose of God that inspired their founding

Fathers." Mr. Dulles is not speaking as a novice in the field of religion as he has been an outstanding Christian lay leader for many years. Many thoughtful lay leaders, as well as Christian ministers, deeply feel that a return to God is absolutely necessary to the survival of mankind.

James Burns, in his book on Revivals, states, "In the history of religion no phenomenon is more apparent than the recurrence of revivals. At certain intervals there sweeps over certain areas and nations a passion of repentance. These revivals when once begun, spread with amazing rapidity. They pervade the atmosphere like a contagion and burst out in unexpected places as if carried by unseen hands."

The current revival did not suddenly appear. It quietly and gradually appeared in many places at the same time, and spread out until it has become a spiritual phenomenon, impressive in its proportions, and deserves top attention from the spiritually minded and the religiously concerned. A spiritual awakening is no longer a devout wish or a fond hope. It is a present reality and apparent to all who have eyes to see, and ears to hear, and hearts to understand. It is crystal clear that it has reached all parts of the country.

The current revival marks a transitional period in our national life as the Renaissance marked the passing of Europe from the medieval to the modern world. The Renaissance passed from Italy where it originated to other European states and expressed itself in different ways in the diverse cultures influenced by it. Just so has the present revival mood found manifold expressions, and proved that it was suited to all degrees of culture, and able to cope with all levels of our national life.

One of our state university presidents recently stated in a public address: "I am more convinced than I have ever been in my life that the greatest need of men is the religion of Christ. The teachings of Jesus are fundamental. His philosophy is the only way of life that will bring ultimate peace and happiness to mankind. We must spread the Christian religion to all the people; we must make disciples for Jesus everywhere."

Many students are in search of God. A few years ago Yale offered a course in Biblical literature which drew only four students. Today the same course draws four hundred students. Fifteen times as many college students are attending church services today as attended a few years ago. Ten years ago one of our large universities employed one chaplain. Today it employs eleven chaplains and several part time workers. A college dean said recently, "I have been in the dean's office for more than twenty years and never have I seen such a wide interest in religion among the students." Many students are findin gGod and are adjusting their lives to his requirements. They are finding solid grounds for their ultimate loyalties, and are taking a fresh look at their Hebrew-Christian heritage.

The present revival has a broader base than any previous revival in the history of our country. There is a heightened spiritual tone in our national capital. The first words spoken by President Eisenhower after his inauguration were, "I ask that you bow your heads," after which he led the nation in prayer. His cabinet meetings open on a prayerful note. A special room for prayer and meditation has been established in the capitol for members of Congress, and it is used by many. It is abundantly evident that many of our statesmen are seeking ideas and inspiration from the Christian tradition to guide them in their political philosophy and legislative attitude. The cynically minded may regard all this as nothing more than political dressing, as "piety on the Potomac." But the serious minded regard it as a religious climate, and as an expression of the renewed spiritual interest all over the country.

The Church of Christ has launched out into the deep and is putting forth extraordinary efforts to make new converts and establish the reign of God. Many soul reaching techniques are being used and revivalism is the order of the day.

The concensus of informed religious opinion is that the church of Christ has experienced a new birth. Tangible results support this opinion. There is an unprecedented attendance at the services of the churches. In many churches it is necessary to hold two Sunday morning services to accomodate the people. Church membership in our country has gone beyond the hundred million mark. Fifty-five hundred new churches have been started since 1953 to provide for the religious needs of this fast-growing population. One denomination has raised eight million dollars for the organization of new congregations and the building of new houses of worship for them.

Our Sunday School facilities are crowded beyond their capacity; the young people of our churches are demonstrating a renewed interest in their work; the work of the women in their organizational life has gone forward by leaps and bounds; family altars have been erected, and there is a new sense of Christian stewardship in its manifold expressions. Increased social service and a heightened missionary concern also register the revival trends and results.

Foot-ball stadiums and other places that accomodate large gatherings are filled with those who are hungry for the word of God. Religious speakers are reaching enormous congregations with their gospel messages as they speak on television and the radio. Our seminaries are overflowing with dedicated young people who are preparing for the Christian ministry and other forms of Christian service.

It is easily seen that the genuineness of the present revival is attested by its fruits. Millions have accepted Christ and found a new life in God. They have become a vital part of the Christian fellowship and good stewards of the manifold grace of God. Many of these new converts are vigorous witnesses for Christ. The Church has risen to new heights in the thought of men and it is more profoundly appreciated than ever before. The dynamic and creative force of the gospel of Christ has been re-established among us. Religion has made a startling comeback. We are in the midst of a major revival movement, and are finding a joyful Christian experience. What has taken place has been given immense publicity, and there is a general awareness that God has again visited our land. We should not be surprised at this visitation for the history of the church is full of examples of the work of the Holy Spirit, and the conversion of masses, sometimes of thousands, as on the day of Pentecost.

When Catherine Marshall, author of "best sellers" was interviewed on television during the Christmas holidays by Edward R. Murrow, she declared that we were living in an "age of spiritual hunger." Mr. Murrow heartily agreed with her when she expressed the belief that this hunger was due to the fact that materialism had failed, that material plenty and comforts had not met the deeper needs of human personality.

Several other causes have been assigned for the wide-spread religious concern—the atom bomb, communism, psychological distress and disillusionment with temporal goals. Doubtless, these are contributing causes, but St. Augustine with his penetrating spiritual insight, underscored the real cause of our discontent when he declared "Thou madest me for Thyself, and my heart is restless until it repose in Thee."

A long time ago, God spoke to men through the prophet Isaiah: "Ho, every one who thirsts, come to the waters; and he who has no money, come, buy and eat! Come, buy wine and milk without money and without price. Why do you spend your money for that which is not bread, and your labor for that which does not satisfy?"

John, in the Book of Revelation, writes to a luke-warm church, "For you say, I am rich, I have prospered, and I need nothing; not knowing that you are wretched, pitiable, poor, blind, and naked."

Jesus directed attention to the basic need of humanity in one of the Beatitudes, "Blessed are those who hunger and thirst for righteousness, for they shall be satisfied." And Jesus said to the woman at Jacob's well in Samaria, "Every one who drinks of this water will thirst again, but whoever drinks of the water that I shall give him will never thirst."

There are divinely implanted longings within the human breast which only God can satisfy. Wells of worldly pleasure, and full troughs of earthly prosperity, and inviting puddles of carnal delight, are always disappointing in the end, and can never take the place of God in meeting and satisfying humanity's fundamental needs.

Revivals of religion in our country have been the inevitable precursors of social and political change. A limitation of space renders it impossible to give a definitive run down on the results of the present revival. But it is obvious that many radical changes have taken place. There is a new spirit of humaneness toward the sufferings, and a quickened conscience regarding injustice; more people are praying and working for world peace and brotherhood than ever before; and during the last several years more remedial and humanitarian legislation has been enacted by our federal and state legislative bodies than in any other like period in the history of our country.

There are doubting Thomases among us who take a dim view of the current revival and doubt that we have experienced a real spiritual awakening. They are not altogether unfriendly to the revival concept. They fear an unfavorable reaction and choose to wait for fuller proof that the revival is genuine and that it will abide. They watch the inflationary spiritual spiral with increasing uneasiness and express the fear that the ancient tribal gods will smother out faith in the true God, and that the latter state will be worse than the first.

These mild critics are skeptical of loud fervor and group hysteria. They believe that much of the religious interest of today is based upon fear of the H-bomb, and mutual annihilation, and is nothing more than a "fox hole religion." They fear that many are trying to use God for their own selfish ends, or to use religion as an outlet for an emotional binge.

It should not be charged that these skeptics are attempting to obscure the real character and purpose of revivalism, or that they are trying by their rather dismal performance to sabotage the current revival. Far from it. They have "honest doubts" and are expressing their views, not to hinder spiritual progress, but to establish a measure of caution.

Collier's Magazine, in an editorial, answers these fears as follows: "The most skeptical observer knows that beneath the occasional crudities and excesses moves a deeper tide, and that for the most part people have turned to religion to increase the moral and spiritual dimensions of their lives."

If Collier's is correct in its analysis, the greatest religious boom in our history is not a shadow without substance, "here today and gone tomorrow, a spiritual bust." History bears eloquent and convincing testimony to the fact that great spiritual awakenings in the past have proved decisive factors in molding the American character and in building our Republic. It is possible that the current revival will strengthen our national character and prepare our people to fulfill our destiny at a crucial time in a fast changing world.

How long will the current revival continue? The law of ebb and flow has always operated in the spiritual realm as it has in the physical, and unless precedent is reversed, the present revival, after it reaches the crest, will be followed by a recession. It may be mild or drastic, depending upon the depth of its penetration into human life. This should be expected and should cause no alarm. In any event, the Church will remain on a high plane of dedication and power. It will never be the same again.

We will need other revivals in the years that lie

ahead. Revivals are not outmoded and we cánnot dispense with them. It is always in order to pray the great revival prayers recorded in the Scriptures: "Wilt Thou not revive us again that Thy people may rejoice in Thee. Revive Thy work O Lord; in the midst of the years make known; in wrath remember mercy."

God's promise made through Solomon to a people in distress should be remembered and cherished by all peoples of earth: "If my people who are called by my name humble themselves, and pray and seek my face, and turn from their wicked ways, then I will hear from heaven, and will forgive their sin, and heal their land."

CHAPTER XIII

THE KIND OF REVIVAL NEEDED

In the preceding chapters the major revivals of all times have been surveyed, their results noted, and the active agents and methods used, have been discussed. In the light afforded by past revivals, we are in a position to consider revivalism as it is related to our present day needs.

A spiritual revival represents the intensified activity of the Christian Church to reach and save the lost. The basic purpose of the church and of the revival is identical. We should never think of them as belonging in separate compartments of life. A refreshing from the presence of the Lord, whenever and however it comes, is the life blood of the church, without which it would soon lose its life giving power. When the Queen of England said, "We cannot rebuild the world without a revival of old fashioned religion," she had in mind that creative religion that flows from our Hebrew-Christian tradition, and that "pure river of water of life, clear as crystal, proceeding out of the throne of God and of the Lamb."

A

WE NEED A REVIVAL THAT COMES FROM GOD

A revival of political interest and business activity can be brought about by the determined action of men, without prayer and dependence upon God. Careful organization and human manipulation will as a usual thing produce the desired results. But human techniques, however faithfully employed, cannot produce a spiritual revival without the inspiring and supporting presence of God.

A few years ago a pretentious evangelistic team was invited to conduct a series of revival services in a rather large city church. It was stipulated in the contract that the evangelists would be paid for their services on the basis of new members received. The team members preached, and sang, and rang door bells for three weeks. The local press gave the services "all out" support, and the interest worked up was city wide. The seating capacity of the large church was taxed to the utmost by the crowds that attended the services.

The campaign was pronounced a huge success. The sponsoring church received several hundred new members, and the evangelists were paid according to contract, and went on their way rejoicing.

But there was something disappointing about the campaign, which was reported by the minister of the church several months later. He sadly confessed that of the hundreds received into his church only six could be located six months after the services closed!

Apparently, this particular revival did not come from God. It had a secular base and was manipulated by men whose dependence was not upon God. The godly minister expressed the conviction that his church was spiritually weaker than before the special services were held.

Those who promote real spiritual revivals lift their eyes to the hills from whence cometh their help. It is God who leadeth sinners to repentance, and it is God who giveth saving faith. Dwight L. Moody would not begin a revival effort until he was sure that prayer cells had been established and were actively supporting the effort. Billy Graham depends quite as much upon supporting prayer in his campaigns as did Mr. Moody. All spiritually minded evangelists know that a favorable revival mood can be created in a church and community only by importunate prayer, and that the organizing of prayer-groups is a matter of supreme importance in a successful revival effort.

All true spiritual revivals that produce abiding results, come from God. They are not worked up and manipulated by human hands and worldly devices. They originate in heaven and come upon communities in answer to conquering prayer. "The prayer of a righteous man has great power in its effects." This observation was made by one of the most realistic and practical Christians, who assisted in writing the New Testament Scriptures.

The Apostle Peter who preached the first sermon after Pentecost, and witnessed the conversion of thousands, referred to revivals as "times of refreshing from the presence of the Lord." From his lonely exile on Patmos, John saw a new heaven and a new earth "coming down from God out of heaven."

B

WE NEED A REVIVAL THAT BRINGS TO MEN
A VIVID SENSE OF GOD

Heart warming sermons, gospel singing, and sincere Christian fellowship, which characterize revival services, are calculated to make those present aware of God. After attending such services many have been heard to say, "God was present in his saving power."

It is true, as we are told in the Letter of James, that a man who observes his natural face in a mirror, may turn away and at once forget what he is like. But a man who beholds God as manifested in Christ does not soon forget what his heart feels and his eyes see of the glory of God. Jacob never forgot the experience he had at the ford Jabbok where he met God and successfully wrestled with his carnal nature until the breaking of the day. After Jacob prevailed in his night-long struggle, he was given a new name, and he had power with God and with men.

The ancient Hebrew prophets and the leaders of the early Christian Church had a keen sense of the presence of God. There was the recognition on their part of a controlling supernatural Being entitled to obedience, reverence, and worship. Their faith in God and deep conviction relative to his presence in the life and affairs of men are forcefully expressed in the following quotations from the Scriptures:

"In the beginning God." "From everlasting to everlasting Thou art God." "Thou God seest me." "It is God with whom we have to do." "Every one shall give an account of himself to God." "It is a fearful thing to fall into the hands of the living God." "God is in this place." "In God we live and move and have our being." "Be still and know that I am God."

The men who wrote these words certainly did not think of God as being obsolete or emeritus and marginal. They thought of God as being alive, active, and relevant. They were piercingly aware of his presence and they were sharply affected by this awareness.

The current revival has quickened our nation's faith in God. We had traveled down the road of God-forgetfulness until we found ourselves on a dead-end street, and without benefit of a detour. Conditions had become so alarming that Walter Lippman wrote in his column, "Unless we rediscover God and a sense of his presence, sheer anarchy awaits us."

A marvelous change has taken place on our national scene. There has been a re-birth of faith in the God of Abraham, Isaac, and Jacob, and in the God and Father of our Lord Jesus Christ.

In our present struggle for survival as a free people, we must look to the God of our salvation for help. "Some boast of chariots, and some of horses; but we boast of the name of the Lord our God. They will collapse and fall; but we shall rise and stand upright." So wrote the Psalmist. Some of the revivals of the past have nerved and strengthened nations in times of crisis, and there is reason to believe that God has sent upon our democracy a gracious revival to prepare us for positive achievement in the cause of peace and a stable world life. The Chaplain of our Senate reflected this belief in his opening prayer at the beginning of the present Congress: "Now, as the world's light fails, we seek the brightness of thy presence, which the black deeds of evil men can never dim."

Faith in God is our first line of defense against the Marxian dialectic from which the very idea of God is excluded. This philosophy of life is atheistic and grossly materialistic, and must be combatted by moral and spiritual ideals resting upon the concept of divine law, and the providence of the Creator and Ruler of the Nations. We are engaged in a terrific struggle against principalities and powers, and the rulers of the darkness of this world, and if our faith in God weakens or crumbles, there is no earthly power that can save us from the tragic fate that has befallen other nations. The future of civilization will be determined by the present struggle.

History is cluttered with the wreckage of nations that have denied God. Germany turned from the true God and returned to her ancient tribal deities and as a result her cities were reduced to rubble and her people to slavery. France officially cast God out of her government about a generation ago, and she has not fared so well since. That country has had succession after succession of weak governments, and as this is written, France, the key-stone of European stability and security, is without a stable government, and a strong voice in the affairs of the world. The nation is paralyzed by its constitutional sickness, and petty politics, and irresponsible bickerings, and impotence of the executive power. When the rulers of Russia turned from God to atheism they ran head-on into history, and sooner or later, will experience the destruction that comes upon nations when they forget God.

The people of India have gained their freedom and are looking forward to becoming a great nation in the family of nations. But can India hope to make substantial progress in her national life under her present leader who is an avowed infidel? "Happy is the people whose God is the Lord."

Our founding fathers believed that God and Liberty belonged together, and inspired by this faith they laid the mud-sills of our Republic and started it on the high road of destiny. They considered themselves tools of God to build a great nation. They believed with George Washington that there are "eternal rules of order and right which heaven itself has ordained." It is believed that only men and women who have an active faith in God will be able to keep the Republic on an even keel and enable it to fulfill its divinely appointed mission to the rest of mankind. A spiritual revival that builds up and strengthens our Christian faith, and enlarges our knowledge of the Father, as Jesus taught us to know him, is always in order and always needed.

C

WE NEED A REVIVAL THAT WILL REGENERATE THE HUMAN SPIRIT

The Scriptures clearly teach the necessity of a conversion experience. The different terms used to describe this inner change are too numerous to mention in a brief discussion. Jesus referred to it as a new birth. He gathered all terms together and expressed them in one short sentence when he said to Nicodemus and to all men, "You must be born anew." He teaches, also, in the same connection that as physical birth is necessary to physical life, just so is spiritual birth necessary to spiritual life. Paul declared, "If any one is in Christ, he is a new creation; the old has passed away, behold the new has come."

The regeneration of the human spirit represents the miraculous power of God as it is applied to human need. The twice-born are living miracles of the redeeming grace of God.

Doctor Adolph Harnack of Berlin finally abandoned his effort to empty the New Testament of the supernatural element because he could not get around the miraculous conversion of Paul.

Christianity began with the miracle of the Incarnation,

and men cannot enter Christ's Kingdom without experiencing the miracle of regeneration. A leading scientist recently testified, "As a Christian a miracle has happened to me. It is the miracle of the new birth, which every one of us who is a Christian has experienced."

The early Christian Church taught and preached the Gospel that proved to be the power of God unto salvation in the life of every one who received it. The history of the early Church was written by Luke, and the Acts of the Apostles is a book of conversions. Wherever the early Christians went they made converts and established spiritual colonies.

The Gospel begins its redemptive work in the heart, because out of the heart are the issues of life. In the unregenerated heart may be found impurity, hatred, envy, jealousy, avarice, intolerance, greed, and other evidences of a depraved nature. All the elements of heathenism exist in unregenerated hearts and lie hidden only by a thin crust of civilization and culture. A long time ago the prophet Jeremiah wrote, "The heart is deceitful above all things, and desperately depraved." When John the Baptist appeared to prepare the way of the Lord, he came with an ax in his hands, which he used on the roots of the trees. The Gospel of Christ becomes effective only when it is applied to the inner life of men.

A Christian life cannot be built upon the shifting sands of an unregenerated human nature, and it is certain that a witnessing church cannot be built upon church members who have not been born from above. The magnificent obsession of Jesus was to establish in this world the Kingdom of God upon the lives of regenerated men.

The real measure of the strength and vitality of a

church is determined by those in its membership who have been born of the Spirit, born of God. In many of our churches we desperately need a revival that will make clear the condition of the natural man as that condition is reflected in the Scriptures; and that will make the Gospel live again in its saving power; and that will bring regeneration to the human spirit.

D

WE NEED A REVIVAL THAT WILL
TRANSFORM HUMAN LIFE

Honest commitment to Christ gives a "new look" to life. Jesus said to men, "Follow me, and I will make you." —He promises change of life and newness of outlook to those who become his disciples. He believed that under his touch the bad could become good, and the ugly beautiful. He soon realized that his faith was fully vindicated, for a radical change appeared in the lives of those whom he touched. They became something other than they were before. Bad women became saintly in life, and rough and profane men became gentle and Christ-like.

Paul called this change which Jesus wrought a transformation. The divine work which begins in the heart permeates the whole of one's life and affects the entire personality.

History gives us notable examples of Christ's transforming power. Matthew, a despised tax collector, becomes a faithful disciple of Jesus and the writer of one of the Gospels; a woman of bad reputation followed Jesus and is numbered with the faithful; Paul the persecutor becomes one of Christ's Apostles and martyrs; Augustine, a dissolute man of the world became a devout Christian and able leader; Tolstoy, a selfish wastrel, became an effective witness for Christ; John Newton, a cruel slave trader, became a gentle Christian; and John Bunyan, the profane tinker of Bedford, became God's mouthpiece. Thus it has ever been, and will continue to be to the close of the gospel dispensation. Christ has power on earth to change human life.

As a young man I witnessed the transformation of a large rural community. Revival fires were kindled in a school house, and on family altars, and the celestial fire purified the community's life and made all things new. Old things passed away and a new kind of life appeared. The community experienced a spiritual resurrection.

About a quarter of a century ago a gospel minister by the name of Hiram Frakes, located in a remote mountain section of Kentucky and staked out a claim in the name of Christ. It was a lawless community, dominated by feudists and moonshiners. He went into this community against the persuasion of those who knew the community and feared for his safety. He was repeatedly threatened by the residents of the community; but he feared no evil in this valley of sin and death.

Mr. Frakes started a church, established a school, and set up family altars in several homes. After several years of patient and unselfish service, the entire community was made new. A former moonshine spot became under the touch of Christ a prosperous Christian community. The lives of the people were changed by a vital experience of the transforming Christ.

Professor Rufus Jones writes of the revival under

Mr. Wesley, "It turned water to wine, it brought prodigals home, it raised life out of death, and produced miracles of transformation."

A missionary after representing Christ in Africa for twenty six years says, "The people of the dark continent are being transformed by the influence of Christ."

Someone has said that Japan looks to the Christian religion for a transforming faith and a new way of life. The Japanese people have observed the work of their own Christian Kagawa over the years and they know that the Christian gospel has transforming power.

Michelangelo looked upon a piece of rejected marble which had been cast aside and said, "There is a beautiful figure in the block and I must liberate it." He cleared away the filth that obscured it and brought forth one of the most gorgeous statues in the world. When he was praised for the work in later years, he remarked, "The figure was there; I only released it."

Under the touch of Christ, the Divine Artist, the obscured and almost washed out image of God in sinful men and women, becomes clearly revealed, and they walk among men as new creations. This redeeming and transforming work is carried forward today by Christ's body, the Church. This work rates high priority in heaven, and it should be the controlling motive of every evangelist and Christian worker.

The Methodist revival in England produced marvelous results. It restored to the Christian Church a fervent spirit, evangelistic doctrines, and the activities of the first century church. The scenes of Pentecost were re-enacted. The unquestioned benefits of the revival can be measured in the altered lives, the improved manners and morals, the noble aims produced, and the higher life of society in communities reached by it.

"We are changing the world," chant fanatical Russian communists as they march around the tomb of Lenin in Moscow. From their viewpoint they are doing a good job. They represent organized brutality with grasping and far-reaching tentacles that hold the helpless as fast as the sucker-bearing arms of an octopus. They have succeeded in turning a large part of the world into a huge slave camp.

Professor Toynbee says that "The Christian religion brought a saving faith to a dying civilization." Saving faith is still in the keeping of the church, and when exercised and acted upon, it still produces the regeneration of the human spirit and the transformation of human life. Those who are committed to the concept of salvation through faith in Christ are changing the face of the world and bringing in the reign of God.

Alfred Noyes, the British poet, made a declaration some years ago which all Christians can easily accept: "There is no hope for humanity unless we find all of our answers in the religion of Christ."

E

WE NEED A REVIVAL THAT WILL DRAW A SHARP LINE OF DEMARCATION BETWEEN RIGHT AND WRONG

In his "My Answer" column, Mr. Graham deals with more questions touching the Decalogue than any other single question. This indicates that there is much confusion in the minds of people as to the life pattern that Christians should follow.

There has always been a conflict between Bible morality and that devised by the ingenuity of men. There are two schools of thought today that challenge the moral law of the Hebrew-Christian tradition. British philosopher, Bertrand Russell, declares that "The ultimate source of ethical standards is nothing more solid than individual human desires and emotions." During the Nazi occupation, Existentialism arose in France. This philosophy stresses personal moral decision without dependence upon established moral values.

These philosophies completely ignore the moral code contained in the Ten Commandments, and the social code set forth in the Sermon on the Mount. The great moralities and decencies of life, which have been the salt of the earth and the light of the world, are based upon these teachings. In fighting for these high ethical values we are fighting for the heart and mind, and soul of humanity. Professor Toynbee claims that "History is a continuing struggle between good and evil." Bishop William T. Watkins declares, "We are passing another great divide in human history. It remains to be seen whether humanity will move into a high realm of life or be swept back into the jungle."

If Mr. Russell and others, who determine their own manner of life without assistance from the divine revelation, succeed in debunking our long honored and deeply cherished moral principles which hold the world together, we will move into an era of moral confusion and chaos and drift down the road to darkness and death.

Christians believe that the Decalogue is inflexible and not subject to change by individual whim or majority vote. Right is determined by the immutable moral law of God.

In the moral realm polls and majorities do not decide between right and wrong. This lies within the province of our Creator and Redeemer, and God has spoken.

"History is a voice forever sounding across the centuries the laws of right and wrong." The world is built on moral foundations. In the end it is well with the good and ill with the wrong. The moral law is written on the tablets of eternity. Jesus wrote this law into the human heart. The Christian does not waste time in discussing priorities of moral values. He knows that God's moral law has precedence over all other expressions of life, and he is forever invoking moral principle.

The Decalogue comprehends the whole compass of moral duty. It enjoins certain kinds of actions and forbids others. There is a moral code binding upon those who profess to live by the Scriptures, and which in the words of Cicero, "Is not subject to man's repeal, suspension, or amendment." God, who is the executive of the moral universe, has drawn a sharp line of demarcation between right and wrong, good and evil, truth and falsehood, holiness and wickedness, and it is not within the power of man to erase this line. God has established a set of values, a measurement of ethical excellence and moral worth, for all time to come, and individuals and nations that ignore these standards, invite disaster and destruction. Our Republic is based upon these values, and if we compromise or depart from them "a creeping dry rot will gnaw at the heart of the nation."

At a recent meeting of a large labor union, Walter Reuther stirred his listeners by appealing for high ethical standards in all their dealings. Elderly statesman Herbert Hoover was eternally right when he declared a short time ago, "A nation is made great by the character and moral fiber of its individual citizens; nations die when these weaken."

Our political leaders declare that religion is vital to our national welfare. President Eisenhower in a recent address to a large group of Christian laymen, said, "We must have a moral and faithful basis of our national behavior to deserve the divine guidance we need." Governor Adlai Stevenson said to the same group, "I believe the Christian faith has been the most significant single element in our history and our tradition. It is our protection against the moral confusion which is too often the moral nihilism of this age."

The New Testament teaching leaves no doubt as to what a sinner is to do in order to be saved, and it also sets forth the nature of the saved life. There is as much emphasis upon the nature of the saved life as there is upon salvation itself. Paul was anxious that Christian believers express a new quality of life, that they be Christ-like in their behavior. The early Christians ever had before them high standards of life, and they were distinguished for their high moral ideals and ethical conduct.

A recent survey of five thousand New York High School students showed that two-thirds of them had never heard of the Ten Commandments! Jewish and Christian leaders have failed to provide a large majority of their young people with ethical foundations for their lives. We cannot believe that this tragic condition prevails throughout the nation. However, it is apparent that throughout the country, rabbis and pastors, evangelists and parents, Christian teachers and responsible leaders, are in a large measure failing to provide Christian nurture and religious training for the youth of our land.

There is an urgent need of a revival of high ethical conduct in all spheres of our life. We need a nation wide revival of religion that will cause the people to return to the Ten Commandments as interpreted by Jesus in the Sermon on the Mount.

F

WE NEED A REVIVAL THAT WILL STRENGTHEN THE CHURCH

Billy Graham believes that "The success of a revival is measured by the number who are converted and become loyal and active members of the church." This measurement of a successful revival is good and acceptable as far as it goes, but it does not go far enough.

Many of our church members came into the church without a conversion experience, and a heart warming revival will often bring them in touch with what is vital in religion. This is especially true of many who unite with the church when of tender age. The great preacher, Horace Bushnell, as a child was exposed to Christian nurture and reared in a godly home, yet he was not converted until he was a college student. This experience came to him during revival services in the college. It is often true in a heart stirring revival that church members make their first discovery of Christ as their personal Savior.

Apart from new members received, a spiritual revival does something significant for the church. The backsliders are reclaimed, the indifferent or marginal members are brought back to the center of the church's life, and the lukewarm are awakened from their slumbers. Pastors of churches where revivals are held have their hearts warmed and are made to rejoice as they see their churches coming alive.

Sometimes a special series of services are conducted in churches with the expressed purpose of "deepening the Christian experience" of the members. Services of this type are directed toward the complete commitment of the lives of the members to Christ. These services, when successful, lead to a rebirth of the churches, and bring the joy and strength of a new dedication.

Spiritual revivals do much to correct the defects of which many Christians are conscious. One of the most successful revivalists of all times, continuously waged a spiritual war against the sub-Christian in himself. Christians can either negotiate a truce with their imperfection and be satisfied with a mediocre Christian life, or they can use all available means of grace, and press forward to appropriate the Christian perfection made possible by the work of Christ and who said to his disciples, "Be you therefore perfect, even as your Father in heaven is perfect."

A hundred Christian laymen met in one of our cities last fall and perfected a plan to train and send out fifteen thousand laymen in a nation-wide effort to bring the unchurched and the unsaved to Christ. It will be a witnessing campaign, and doubtless many converts will be made. But the ultimate test of the work accomplished will be determined by the character of the churches that receive these new converts.

Dr. Albert Schweitzer directs attention to the fact that the object of Protestant missions in Africa is to build Christian personalities; and, he does not believe that this object can be realized without a firmly established church and the ministry of a vital church.

The Epistles of Paul were written to confirm believers in the faith and to guide them toward the realization of Christian maturity. A few weeks after the rise of the Christian movement in Jerusalem, a pattern emerged for looking after the converts. "The Lord added to their number day by day those who were being saved," and those who were added were led to devote themselves to the apostles' teaching and fellowship, and to the breaking of bread and prayers.

John Wesley expressed as much concern in providing means of grace for his many converts as he did in making them. He revived and followed the New Testament pattern. He conserved the effects of the nation-wide revival which he promoted by organizing the converts into societies where they held preaching services, testimony meetings, and love feasts. The converts received individual care from competent leaders and the fruits of the revival were preserved.

Typical reports are as follows: "Large crowds attended every service. A general spiritual awakening has come to the membership of the church." Another writes, "The Church was revived spiritually and several were converted." A pastor observed, "The genuineness of a revival is evidenced in the changed lives of the people and the increased attendance at the services of the church."

According to these statements, revivals should result in the conversion of sinners and the edification of believers. During a revival period church members receive a new sense of the glory and power of their faith, and the gospel net which is thrown out over a community with compelling persuasion draws the unsaved toward the Savior, who is able and willing to pardon their sins.

Spiritual revivals greatly assist in making the "Church big enough for God." "When the world is at its worst, the Church should be at its best." When evil beats upon us like a flood, we as Christians should be in a position to lift high God's standards. When freedom and civilization are threatened on many fronts, and God says, "Where are my people, the Christians?" we should immediately answer, "We are here, we have been alerted, we are standing by."

A revival in a church is a call of God to every member to renew his Christian covenant and to make a complete dedication of his life to the will and purpose of God. A Bishop of one of our large denominations says, "We need a revival in our churches of private and public worship, of Bible reading and church going, and of Christian stewardship."

An evangelistic campaign in a community, however pretentious and costly it may be, is of doubtful value if it does not draw the unsaved to Christ and make the church more vital and meaningful in the life of the community. It is a sad experience for a pastor to find, as is often the case, less spiritual interest in his church after a revival closes than there was before it began.

We need a revival that will re-vitalize the church, and make it what God expects it to be. A seminary president truly observes, "The work of the church is the biggest business in the world because it is the only business which will save the world." In its work of saving the souls of men, the church has no competitor and it has no companion.

While we are rejoicing because of the definite and unmistakable upsurge of religious interest over the country which is manifest in many places and in many different ways, we should not allow our traditional optimism to create among us a mood of over-confidence and cause us to make overstatements as to the final results. There followed emperor Constantine into the Christian Church a large influx of members who proved a liability and not a help to the church. This could happen again. Eternal vigilance is necessary to spiritual success. There is much religious illiteracy in the church and many spiritual babes, and we must have at once an intensified program of religious education, and a Christian leadership training program, that will develop greater skill in teaching religion.

> *"Come, Holy Spirit, heavenly Dove,*
> *With all thy quickening powers;*
> *Kindle a flame of sacred love*
> *In these cold hearts of ours."*